The Autobiography of

The Little Girl from

Andersonville

1949-2017
You Can Make It through the Hurricane

RHODESSIA STRONG

ISBN 978-1-0980-2572-4 (paperback)
ISBN 978-1-0980-6174-6 (hardcover)
ISBN 978-1-0980-2573-1 (digital)

Christian Faith Publishing, Inc.
832 Park Avenue
Meadville, PA 16335
www.christianfaithpublishing.com

Printed in the United States of America

DEDICATION

First and foremost, I give thanks and praise to our almighty Father for the precious gift of life and wisdom. Second, I dedicate this book to the late Elder Samuel John Strong Jr. who labored so faithfully, assisting in typing and proofing my papers during the years of *acquiring both* bachelor's and master's degrees. He sacrificed a lot, physically, *mentally*, and *financially*, *motivating* me to pursue my dreams as a marriage and family therapist, as well as my vision in ministry. How can I forget thirty-two years, six months, eight days, and sixteen hours of a *wonderful* marriage *we shared together*, the good times and not-so-good times, the joy serving God together in ministry, and serving others in and out of the ministry—I don't think I will forget our last smiley conversations the day you left me! Your labor was not in vain. You should hear: "Well done thou good and faithful servant." I have fought a good fight, I have finished my course, I have kept the faith: 2 Timothy 4:7 King James Version (KJV)

To my daughter Sandie Renea and my son Samuel John III, you both made us proud parents. Some of your dad's words, the night before he *transitioned* to heaven, were: "I am very proud of Sandie and Sam." He was very pleased that God had allowed him to live to see you both become responsible and independent young adults.

To my other precious family members—too many to name—to Solid Rock Redemptive Ministries, and ministry supporters, especially Ministers Brenda Bell, Cynthia English, Tabitha Steven-Allen, and Debra Kemp, and *Pure Vessels of God (PVOG)*. Your labor was not in vain! *In all you do, acknowledge God and he will direct your path.*

May God continue to shower you all with blessings!!!

Love,
Rhodessia "Rose" Strong.

CONTENTS

PREFACE

I was motivated to write my story of courage, love, hope, compassion, and strength that will not only teach and inspire others to follow the paths of righteousness but also encourage me to continue standing up *for what is true and noble* and trusting God, knowing that he will never leave me nor forsake me.

ACKNOWLEDGMENTS

In all thy ways acknowledge him,
and he will direct your path.

—Proverbs 3:6

First, I give thanks to the almighty God for keeping me safe through life's challenges. Had not God been on my side, I would not be alive today. Reflecting back on my life from childhood, I know only God could have brought me through the many *"hurricanes" in my life.*

I thank God for those whom he had placed in my life to pray and fast with me, encouraged me, and spoke positive words to me during some difficult times. You all were very awesome prayer warriors during those days! Special thanks to my brothers: Joseph and his late wife, Ann; Ruben and his late wife, Annie, Dr. Mary L. Thompson, Mr. and Mrs. Council Ingram, Sr. and family, Brenda Bell, and so many others who continue—you were all there standing in the gap with me. Last, but not least, a special thank-you to Ella Williams of SME Business Services, Inc. who labored tireless with me in editing this autobiography. May God continue to shower everyone with his richest blessings.

The Autobiography of
The Little Girl from Andersonville
1949-2017
"You Can Make It Through the Hurricane"

By: Rhodessia "Rose" Strong

INTRODUCTION

I must say, if you are righteous, expect to go through storms, winds, trials, troubles, and others. However, when we are tested, cling to God!

Do not lean on what you feel, think, or assume. Proverbs 3:5–6 (GW) says, "Trust the *Lord* with all your heart, and do not rely on your own understanding. In all your ways acknowledge him, and he will make your paths smooth."

In Psalm 23:4 (GW), it is said, "Even though I walk through the dark valley of death, because you are with me, I fear no harm. Your rod and your staff give me courage." Simply put—do not fear—for God is with you!

The storms of life were created to help us grow stronger and to help us draw closer to God. Thunderstorms, winds, trials, and tests do not come to stay; they will pass. As the Psalmist reminds us: "Many are the afflictions of the righteous: but the Lord delivereth him (your name) out of them all (trials, tests, and troubles too").

> I've told you this so that my peace will be with you. In the world you'll have trouble. But cheer up! I have overcome the world. (John 16:33, GW)

After Job prayed for his friends, the *Lord* restored Job's prosperity and gave him twice as much as he had before.

Then all his brothers and sisters and everyone who had previously known him came to him. They ate with him at his house, sympathized with him, and comforted him for all the evil the *Lord* had brought to him. Each one gave him some money and a gold ring.

The *Lord* blessed the latter years of Job's life more than the earlier years. He had 14,000 sheep and goats, 6,000 camels, 2,000 oxen, and 1,000 donkeys.

He also had seven sons and three daughters.

He named the first {daughter} Jemimah, the second Cassia, and the third Keren Happuch.

Nowhere in the whole country could be found women who were as beautiful as Job's daughters. Their father gave them and their brothers an inheritance.

Job lived 140 years after this. He saw his children, grandchildren, and great-grandchildren.

Then at a very old age, Job died. (Job 42:10–17, GW)

I encourage you to not allow the thunderstorms, the winds, hurricanes, trials, tests, and troubles of life draw you away from God. Instead, cling, draw, pull, hold on, and do not give up, because God will not leave you—he will not let you fall. He will hold you up with his right hand of righteousness. Therefore, I urge you to do what Job did in the midst of his *hurricane* season—Job worshipped God.

Job 1:20 (GW) says, "Job stood up, tore his robe in grief, and shaved his head. Then he fell to the ground and *worshiped*."

After all Job had been through, he did not give up on God, neither did he blame God for his captivity. *Instead, he worshipped.* Next, Job prayed for his friends. "Someone would say: 'I would pray for myself. After all, I am the one in trouble!'" Job found strength, encouragement, and endurance when he prayed for his friends.

> And the Lord turned the captivity of Job, when he prayed for his friends: also the Lord gave Job twice as much as he had before. (Job 42:10)

While he prayed for others, the Lord turned his captivity into victory! Job had twice as much as he had in the beginning of his *hurricane* season. He (Job) was more than a conqueror through it all—through him that love him, almighty God. God gave Job double for his trouble—this should be encouraging to you. Because Job endured all the storms, winds, and rain, during his hurricane, the Lord *greatly* blessed Job.

So I encourage you to hold on "child of God"—your greater is on the way!!!

Who is tested? Some of God's chosen peoples in the Bible were tested but did not give up or quit. Here are a few examples: During his times of testing, King David sought refuge from the Lord, through meditation, as follows:

> The Lord tests righteous people, but he hates wicked people and the ones who love violence. (Psalms 11:5, GW)

> Examine me, O Lord, and test me. Look closely into my heart and mind. (Psalms 26:2, GW)

> The righteous person has many troubles, but the Lord rescues him from all of them. (Psalms 34:19, GW)

> The victory for righteous people comes from the Lord. (Psalms 37:39, GW)

> Examine me, O God, and know my mind. Test me, and know my thoughts. See whether I am on an evil path. Then lead me on the everlasting path." David asked God to search him! (Psalms 139:23–24, GW)

Isaiah 43:1–4 (GW) says:

> The Lord created Jacob and formed Israel. Now, this is what the Lord says: "Do not be afraid, because I have reclaimed you. I have called you by name; you are mine. When you go through rivers, they will not sweep you away. When you walk through fire, you will not be burned, and the flames will not harm you. I am the Lord your God, the Holy One of Israel, your Savior. Egypt is the ransom I exchanged for you. Sudan and Seba are the price I paid for you. Since you are precious to me, you are honored and I love you. I will exchange others for you. Nations will be the price I pay for your life."

Am I saying God caused *trials or tribulations* in my life, in your life? No, not at all! The God we serve is a loving, caring, compassionate God. He knows what we will encounter in this earthly life. In the meantime, he says in his word in Hebrews 13:5 (GW): "Don't love money. Be happy with what you have because God has said, 'I will never abandon you or leave you.'"

What Is a Hurricane—In the Natural?

According to Merriam Webster Dictionary, a "hurricane" is defined as: "An extremely large, powerful, and destructive storm, with very strong winds that occur especially in the western part of the Atlantic Ocean."

In the natural, just as the tropical system assigns a category, depending on the speed of the wind and what those winds will likely do once the system makes landfall, the tropical system warns us of what is about to happen.

In the spiritual system, God warns those who believe, trust, love, *obey,* and serve him in righteousness, *in spirit and truth.* He does not tell us what those trials, tests, troubles, and afflictions would be; however, Apostle Paul warns believers:

> For this reason *I suffer as I do.* However, I'm not ashamed. I know whom I trust. I'm convinced that He is able to *protect* what he had entrusted to me until that day. (2 Timothy 1:12, GW)

> You also know about the kind of <u>persecutions and sufferings</u> which happened to me in the cities of Antioch, Iconium, and Lystra. I endured those *persecutions,* and the Lord *rescued me* from all of them.
>
> Those who try to live a godly life because they believe in Christ Jesus *will be persecuted.* Paul did not give up! (2 Timothy 3:11–12, GW)

> *Blessed are those who endure* when they are tested. *When they pass the test, they will receive*

the crown of life that God has promised to those who love him. (James 1:12, GW)

God, who shows you his kindness and who has called you through Christ Jesus to his eternal glory, *will restore you, strengthen you, make you strong, and support you as you suffer for a little while.*

Power belongs to him forever. Amen.

I've written this short letter to you and I'm sending it by Silvanus, whom I regard as a faithful brother. I've written to encourage you and to testify that this is God's genuine good will. Remain firmly established in it! (1 Peter 5:10–12, GW)

Think of what Jesus our Lord and savior encountered—too much for any believer to bear—but Jesus did not give up, because he knew he had a purpose. So he bore his cross. Our tests, trials, troubles, persecutions, or sufferings cannot be compared to what Jesus went through for us. Jesus said:

Blessed are those who are persecuted for doing what God approves of. The kingdom of heaven belongs to them.

Blessed are you when people insult you, persecute you, lie, and say all kinds of evil things about you because of me.

Rejoice and be glad because you have a great reward in heaven! (Matthew 5:10–12)

The prophets who lived before you were persecuted likewise. The apostle Paul gives the assurance in Romans 8:35–39 (KJV):

Who shall separate us from the love of Christ? *Shall* tribulation, or distress, or persecution, or famine, or nakedness, or peril, or sword?

As it is written, for thy sake we are killed all the day long; we are accounted as sheep for the slaughter.

Nay, in all these things we are more than conquerors through him that loved us.

For I am persuaded, that neither death, nor life, nor angels, nor principalities, nor powers, nor things present, nor things to come,

Nor height, nor depth, nor any other creature, shall be able to separate us from the love of God, which is in Christ Jesus our Lord. So *rejoice!!!*

The Purpose for Sharing My Autobiography

I believe what Jesus said in John 8:54 (GW):

> If I bring glory to myself, my glory is nothing. My Father is the one who gives me glory, and you say that He is your God.

I desire to share some of my life's winds, storms, hurricanes, etc., that I have encountered and how I overcame them. I did not give up—rather, I held on to God—and he kept me through them all! Although, it is the norm to continue to encounter some winds, storms, etc. (in everyday life), I know God is faithful in keeping his promises.

I want to encourage others who are still going through their winds or storms or will go through some storms in their life, especially those new believers in Christ, those who feel there is no help or hope, or those who feel God is not with them. Because of challenges, many *people* turn away from God's truth. However, I encourage you to continue to stand, and when you have done all you know to do, according to God's Word, keep standing, believing, declaring his Word, and trusting him.

> The *Lord* created Jacob and formed Israel. Now, this is what the *Lord* says: Do not be afraid, because I have reclaimed you. I have called you by name; you are mine.
>
> When you go through the sea, I am with you. When you go through rivers,

they will not sweep you away. When you walk through fire, you will not be burned, and the flames will not harm you.

I am the *Lord* your God, the Holy One of Israel, your Savior. Egypt is the ransom I exchanged for you. Sudan and Seba are the price I paid for you.

Since you are precious to me, you are honored and I love you. I will exchange others for you. Nations will be the price I pay for your life.

Do not be afraid, because I am with you. I will bring your descendants from the east and gather you from the west. (Isaiah 43:1–5, GW)

What God promised Jacob is for his children who put their trust in Him. You are more than a conqueror (Romans 8:37, GW).

Instead, focus on what the Apostle Paul said in Romans 8:31–39 (GW):

What can we say about all of this? If God is for us, who can be against us?

God didn't spare his own son but handed him over (to death) for all of us. So he will also give us everything along with him.

Who will accuse those whom God has chosen? God has approved of them.

Who will condemn them? Christ has died, and more importantly, he was brought back to life. Christ has the highest position in heaven. Christ also intercedes for us.

What will separate us from the love Christ has for us? Can trouble, distress, persecution, hunger, nakedness, danger, or violent death separate us from his love?

As the scripture says: "We are being killed all day long because of you. We are thought of as sheep to be slaughtered."

The one who loves us gives us an overwhelming victory in all these difficulties.

I am convinced that nothing can ever separate us from God's love which Christ Jesus our Lord shows us. We can't be separated by death or life, by angels or rulers, by anything in the present or anything in the future, by forces.

Or powers in the world above or in the world below, or by anything else in creation.

God is with "you," so stand up on your tiptoes, and stretch your hands as far as you can, as if you are reaching for gold or money falling from the sky. Then give God praise and thanks for bringing you through past challenges.

CHAPTER 1

The Little Girl from Andersonville

You Can Make It through the Hurricane

It started here.

Mollie Stephens was born to her parents Mollie Edge and Clarence Stephens on March 3, 1911. Clarence Stephens was of Indian descent, dark complexion with long black curly hair, rode a horse, smoked a pipe, and made barbecue for the plantation owners. He was married to Mollie Edge whose complexion was high yellow with long red hair. Mollie was the second to last of her siblings. Mollie explained that one night the Klu Klux Klan came and forcefully snatched Clarence away. They beat him very badly that night and, as a result, Clarence became extremely incapacitated. Due to his emotional condition, Clarence was unbearably strict, thus, causing some of the older siblings to leave home early and migrate to other cities and states. Mollie's dream of becoming a school teacher was also shattered due to the devastating events of her father. She eventually had to drop out of high school to assist her mother in caring for her father who later died from complications of the injuries he sustained from the beatings. Information on Mollie Edge-Stephens' death is unknown.

After the death of her father, Mollie later met and married Cleo Baldwin. They both were very young, in their mid-teens. There was no information on the history of Cleo Baldwin, except being known as the brother of Clara Baldwin-McDonald. From this union, seven children were born to Mollie Stephens-Baldwin and Cleo Baldwin, consisting of four girls (Catherine, Mollie-Ruth, Bobbie, and Doris) and three boys (Ruben, Leo, and Clem). There was a miscarriage between the oldest sibling Catherine and the twins Ruben and Mollie-Ruth. Unfortunately, Cleo was incarcerated for selling moonshine (whiskey). During this time, he was hospitalized and died of a heart attack in 1943.

At a very young age, suddenly, Mollie became a widow and single parent who had no other choice but to completely revamp her lifestyle. Having no choice, she quickly reorganized family roles and rules among her seven children. Still, the family's responsibilities weighed heavily on her shoulders. There was no life insurance available at the time of her husband's death, leaving her to take care of the seven children on her own.

The Mother Who Would Not Give Up

Mother did not depend on others for help—I do not ever recall her asking for or getting assistance from anyone—of course, there were no government programs to aid those in need.

Her only available resources were monies earned from working on the plantation—and sometime borrowed money from the plantation owners which she would pay back later—and clothes that were given by extended family members. My older brother moved to Miami, Florida in 1956 and later my oldest sister who had a son, leaving him back home with mother. They would send mother money when they could.

Seven years later, still a young woman, mother had four additional children plus a grandson belonging to her oldest daughter to care for on her own. She had a miscarriage between the second and third child. I remembered when times were very hard and we had very little. As a plantation worker, mother worked in the fields chopping and picking cotton, peas, and peaches, shaking peanuts, picking up pecans, shucking corn, and picking blackberries. She also worked at a canning plant where they canned many food products. Many days mother would work from early morning until sunset. She earned minimum wages of fifteen dollars a week chopping cotton. The most money earned was from picking cotton, peaches, pecans, and corn because they were weighted by the pound. On the other hand, mother always had a way to make ends meet.

To ensure that the family always had food, mother did not hesitate to put in action her God-given wisdom. She had a separate area on her property where she planted different vegetables—cabbage, collards, mustard, turnip greens, peas, sweet potatoes, green onions, okra, tomatoes, squash, cucumbers, hot peppers, watermelon, and sugar cane. When it was time for meat, mother knew all the wild animals and birds that were good to be eaten (rabbits, squirrels, possums, and birds). Being such a good cook, the way mother seasoned and simmered those meats, one could hardly tell the difference.

Mother was also a very multitalented individual. She made small throw rugs from old stockings and quilts from scraps of fabrics by hand (between the late thirties or early forties—only one quilt remaining, and hopefully will be placed in a quilt Museum in Florida). She baked cakes, sweetbread, and sweet egg bread—yummy! The three- or four-layer chocolate cake and the lemon cheese and pineapple cake were the bomb! She also made sweet potato pie, blackberry and peach gobble, egg custard, cornbread turkey, and chicken dressing that no one could top! Oh my—how could I forget!!! When we could not afford to buy cold drinks/soda pops or even a bottle of grape or strawberry Kool-Aid, she made sweetened water (sugar and water mixed together, add a slice of lemon—now we call it lemonade). Mother was, indeed, a survivor. She was an expert when it came to making potash soap from hog scraps. However or whatever she made it from, it surely cleaned and whitened our clothes.

She was a genius when it came to canning and storing foods for the winter and hard times; she canned peaches, blackberries, pears, and peas.

Looking through the eyes of wisdom, mother made preserves from watermelon rinds. Oh, the pear preserves were to die for. If you don't believe me, ask my brother Joe—LOL!!! Ironically, mother raised her own chickens and hogs; at times, she would kill a hog and preserve the meat for almost a year. Not wasting any part, she made souse from pig ears, pig feet, and pig tails.

In those days, we had no refrigerator, just a little ice-box. Today, that is called a cooler. Mother would buy a block of ice and wrap it in a wool cloth. The ice lasted for days, keeping food from spoiling. One thing mother did that really amazed me was when she dug a hole in the ground, lined the hole with pine straws, placed sweet potatoes inside and then covered it with several more layers of straws. She covered the hole with a wooden board or tin which kept the potatoes fresh for months.

Although she never taught her children about slavery and how black people (in general) were treated in earlier times, it was not long before we realized that prejudice and slavery were a fact of life then, especially for blacks. On one occasion, I recalled me and my sister taking the bus to Americus to look around. On our journey, we stopped at the window of a small restaurant to buy hamburgers. As we approached the front window, the attendant immediately ordered us to go to the back window. In another instance, on our way home while waiting at the bus station, I went into the restroom. Totally unaware of segregation, differentiating "whites" from "colored," I could see the hateful resentment on the white women's faces, staring at me as if I had committed a crime—I said nothing! When we got on the bus, I also recalled not sitting at the back of the bus, either. As a teen, I realized I was very bold during those times—was I—or was I living under God's protective hands? I would say the latter!

Mollie's new life in Christ

In the late 1950s, at the age of nine or ten, one night, I recalled two of our neighbors visiting with Mollie. They all sat together in front of the fireplace; they were talking about God. Curious to learn more about God, while my other siblings went to bed, I sat around the fireplace with them trying to understand what they were saying. As I reflected, it could have been a prayer meeting. Suddenly, Mollie yelled out crying. She shouted, "Thank you, Jesus, yes! Thank you, master!" She continued speaking in a strange language, and that was a great early-life experience for me as a little girl. This was the beginning of Mollie's new life in Christ.

She was baptized and joined the Mt. Calvary Primitive Baptist Church in Andersonville—they held services once a month. She believed the Holy Bible to be true and inspired by God (2 Timothy 3:15–17). However, the life she displayed was proof that she was truly a born-again believer in Christ Jesus. After moving to Miami, Florida, Mollie moved her membership to Mt. Mary Primitive Baptist Church in Fort Lauderdale, Florida, where she remained faithful until death on August 16,1997.

What's the meaning of Rhodessia?

- Righteous, rich, and rooted in God
- Honest, holy, and humble
- Overcomer in Christ Jesus
- Devoted to God, husband, and family

- Evangelistic and equipped in God
- Servant of the highest God
- Strong in the Lord and in the power of his might
- Intercessor, invading the kingdom of the devil
- After the heart of God

Favorite colors

- Blue: heavenly
- Gold: perfection and integrity
- Ivory: wealth and luxury
- Purple: royalty
- White: purity, victory, and completion and God's glory
- Red: love, boldness, and strength
- Sage green: nature and light

Interests

- God's perfect and divine will be fulfilled in my life.
- Reaching the total man regardless of religion, gender, or race.

THE AUTOBIOGRAPHY OF RHODESSIA BALDWIN

"The Little Girl From Andersonville"

Where is Andersonville?

Andersonville is a city in Sumter County, Georgia, USA. As of the 2010 census, the city had a population of 255. It is located in the southwest part of the state, approximately sixty miles southwest of Macon on the center of Georgia railroad. During the American Civil War, it was the site of a prisoner-of-war camp, which is now Andersonville National Historic Site. (Please Google for more information.)

From birth to age five

I was told, it was springtime, on a windy day, Monday, March 23, 1949, in Andersonville, Georgia, that Dr. Derek, M.D. delivered a gorgeous baby girl to Mollie Stephens-Baldwin and, father, Ruffs Minus. I am the eighth of eleven children born to Mollie. I understand there were some disagreement as to what Mollie would name this gorgeous little baby girl. My oldest brother suggested, "You should name her Snow Pearl?" I'm sure that Mollie looked at her beautiful baby girl and said, "Oh no! I'm going to name her Rodeasa?" On my birth certificate, the spelling of my name was "Rodeasa." In my late teens, I corrected the spelling to reflect "Rhodessia." The name "Rhodessia" means *successful and joyful.* In numbers, "Rhodessia" means eight. Biblically, the number eight means new beginnings. I wish I would have asked my Mollie how she came up with that name. Looking back on that day, she spoke prophetically over me. Presumably, I was a pretty healthy baby. I don't recall my Mollie telling me of any difficulties or illnesses I had as an infant.

Website reflections on the meaning of the name "Rhodessia"

- You are a law unto itself.
- Your tendency is to finish whatever you start.
- You are tolerant and like to help humanity.
- You are very active.
- You are generally warmhearted and gives freely of your time and energy.
- You have sympathetic understanding.
- You have tolerance and acceptance of the frailties of others.
- You are universal and humanitarian in outlook.
- This is a very compassionate name.
- You are frank and methodical and believe in law, system, and order.
- You are very intuitive.

- You have a reservoir of inspired wisdom combined with inherited analytical ability, which could reward you through expressions of spiritual leadership, business analysis, marketing, artistic visions, and scientific research.
- Operating on spiritual side of your individuality can bring you to the great heights and drop you off if you neglect your spiritual identity.
- You are always looking for an opportunity to investigate the unknown, to use and show your mental abilities, and to find the purpose and meaning of life.
- You want to grow wise and to understand people and things.
- You need privacy to replenish your energy.
- You have a unique way of thinking and are intuitive, reflective, and absorbing.

CHAPTER 2

One Teacher, Several Groups

Pre-K

I am not sure what age I was when I went to elementary school, maybe five or six years old. I recalled the joy of going to school in a little church with only one teacher, accountable for teaching children of different ages and groups in one classroom. Symmetrically, the teacher would teach one group and have them go over practicing the lesson while she worked with the next group. I could still visualize myself sitting in a circle with other children, hair in three ponytails with ribbons tied in a petty bow on each, neatly ironed dress with a large tie in the back, white socks, and black shoes—looking so pretty—with a little old book, reading aloud saying my *ABCs*!!! Thank you, mother, for doing so much to afford me an education—I will always cherish these moments.

Elementary Shy but Eternally Grateful

Looking back, as the little girl from Andersonville, entering elementary school was somewhat of an emotional time for me, not knowing any of the children. Seemingly, the teachers had no problem teaching the students. There were times when some students would be invited to go to the teachers' homes where they would receive extra help with homework assignments. In those days, students had to line up for lunch—a tradition which continues in today's schools. I recalled lunches at the cafeteria were only $.20/day, $1.00/week. However, mother just could not afford even the $.20/day, so she prepared lunch for me which I carried in a little brown paper bag. By lunchtime, the grease from the meats had soaked through the bag. Nonetheless, I held the bag up close to my mouth to eat so that the children could not see what my lunch consisted of.

On the contrary, as I sat at the table with other students, I was able to see what they were having for lunch. Often times, their lunches consisted of beefaroni, Jell-o, fruit cocktail, rolls, and a little carton of milk. There were days when I had cornbread and fried sweet potatoes or cornbread *and a piece of fat back or streak of lean meat.* Although some students were curious or inquisitive, wanting to see what was in my "little brown bag," thankfully, I don't recall anyone making fun of me. At times, I felt a little ashamed, but at least I had something to eat, and I considered that a great blessing because of what my mother was going through. Mother had many children to provide for, her four, plus a grandson from my oldest sibling.

Despite the odds, I recalled how excited I became wanting to participate in my first graduation program. Unfortunately, my mother could not afford to buy me a costume. However, I could just see her beaming with pride—and thinking out loud—*Come what may, my child is going to participate in this graduation!!!* So she bought some crepe paper from which she made my costume. I did not recall us having a rehearsal, but I do remember entering the stage on the day of the program with other children and sitting in a circle.

From that day onward, I learned a valuable lesson. My mother wanted me to be unique, because she, too, was a unique person. From that time, the launching of my creative abilities for sewing, fashion designing, and decorating began, up until this day. It was after this event/graduation I recall sometime later or should I say the next school year the children were bused to a larger school with separate classrooms, maybe individual grades at that time.

Starting Work at a Very Young Age

At age eleven, as a little girl growing up in Andersonville, Georgia, life was difficult for me. I was the eighth child of eleven children born to my mother. My oldest sister had a son whom she left with my mother to care for, while she and my oldest brother moved to Miami, Florida. They would work and send money to help mother when they could. When there was no school, mother *would take us all to work with her in the fields.* Years later, my older brother brought his son less than a year old to live with us for a while. My job at the time was to stay home and babysit my nephew, which was not easy for this little girl from Andersonville, who was just stepping into puberty stage, with no warning of body changes. After a while, his parents came and took him back to Miami. Not having much of anything to do, rather that moping, I went to work in the fields, picking cotton, peas, and peaches, shaking peanuts, and plucking corn to help mother provide for the rest of the family of six.

Mother had her last child in 1955. At this time, there were no daycare centers or babysitters, so mother had to take all her children to work also. She would find a special area and have the younger siblings sit, keeping a close eye on them and trusting the good master (God) that no snakes would bite them or any other creatures harm them while she worked. Nonetheless, I do remember mother making a little bed about three to four feet from the bottom end of her long cotton sack where she would lay her baby, carefully dragging the sack as she continued picking cotton and putting it in the same sack. Even though she did not complete high school, she was very gifted in reading, writing, math, and science. It was so amazing how the gift of wisdom manifested in her life. Thank God, her legacy continues to manifest in me. Hopefully, this legacy will continue in the family through many generations.

Education was a must

My middle to high school years was the bomb! Meanwhile, we were bused to school in *Americus*, Georgia, which was approximately ten or more miles from my home on Freedman Hill. It was fun walking with other children for a mile or two to wait for the bus to pick us up. I looked forward to PE—changing into my PE uniform consisting of black shorts almost to the knee, white socks, and white sneakers. As a team, we played basketball, jump rope, or track and field and meet and interact with students from other communities.

Our mother did her very best to send us to school to learn, and we, in turn, put forth our best effort to absorb. We had no brand-named shoes or clothes, only one pair of shoes for school which was the penny loafer or black-and-white Oxford shoes and one or two pairs of socks for the school year, not to mention clothing. Our relatives sent us clothing from other states. We did not have a lot of clothes—sometimes we wore the same clothing for two or three days. When I got home from school, I took off my school clothes and hang them up and put them back on the next day. I remember when my mother would wash and straighten my hair with Apex hair oil and then braid it up. We had no weaves, just our natural hair—three ponytails, sometimes a little bangs, one ponytail on top and one on each side, with little bows or ribbons on the end or over the rubber band.

Despite the difficulties, those were some great times during my life. However, the knowledge and wisdom that I gained through those life experiences has helped me immensely to appreciate the love, care, hard work, and perseverance of our mother who gave so much so that her children could have a better chance at life than she did.

My older siblings Ruben, Catherine, and Bobbie were living in Miami, Florida. In the late 1950s or early 1960s, my second oldest brother Leo, his wife, and three children also moved to Miami, Florida, in search of better opportunities. My sister Doris also moved to Miami earlier, between 1961 and 1962.

Back then, we had no cellphones. Once school was out, we all went back to our small towns. There were very few children living in our neighborhood. Along with my three siblings and a nephew, there were approximately twelve other children around my age group and younger. With the exception of one girl who dropped out of school after getting pregnant, I did not recall any fighting at school.

During those days, students were very respectful to teachers—no disrespect or doing your own thing was tolerated. It is a known fact that when one tries to do good, evil always presents itself. Despite trying to keep the peace, I must say I was involved in one serious fight which, believe me, I tried very hard to avoid—and I was not the initiator. This wild "bully" kept picking on me, knocking my books out of my hands, stepping on my foot, pointing up in my face, and brushing up against me. At this point, I was so heated I grabbed her, and the fight was on. Later, I understood that her sister attempted to help her double-team me, but my brother Joe, my sister Vera, and my nephew Willie said to the bully's sister, "If you help your sister, we are going to help our sister." *It's true where there is unity, there is strength.* I guess the bully's sister was wise. She learned quickly that four is stronger than two.

Knowing my brother Joe, he didn't play. Joe would fight anyone or everyone who contended with him, despite their size or gender. I believe Joe got that from our daddy or one of his older brothers, Leo. It was a known fact that three of my mother's siblings known as the Stephens brothers were fighters—I was told that they were some tough boys—they didn't play. They beat up people like nobody's business, in those days. Evidently, Joe got his boldness, toughness, and being strong-willed from his uncles, the Stephens brothers.

I further understood that my sister Vera was also a fighter—well, she must have gotten hers from one of our mother's sisters. No, we think she got it from our daddy—LOL!!! I believe my sister Vera would have beaten the bully and her sister with one hand. At that time, I am not sure if my nephew was a fighter, but he would have helped. Although my baby brother Lenny was still very young to attend middle school, I believe he, too, would have helped. Thank God for siblings who are not afraid of bullies!!! Among all siblings, there are the occasional sibling rivalries. Still, it is factual that some sibling fights only last for minutes and then they make up. Although my sister Vera, my brother Joe, and my nephew Willie often had sibling fights, we quickly fell back in siblings love. Of course, I always won the bet! We are a pretty close-knit, large family who watches out for one another's backs.

CHAPTER 3

Family Shockwave—Tragedy Struck

Oh, what a dark day it was when tragedy struck in February 1964. We received some devastating news that my second oldest brother, living in Miami at the time, had been killed. I don't recall how mother first received the news, maybe a family member drove from Miami to Andersonville to inform the rest of the family. His body was shipped back and laid to rest in Freeman Hill Cemetery in Andersonville. After the funeral, most of the family members returned to Miami, with the exception of one family member who stayed behind with her newborn baby girl. It was, indeed, very painful for everyone. I was too young to understand the grief and loss mother was going through losing a child. In shock, I do recall thinking and even dreaming about my brother. I was about fourteen years old at the time. Our family was in shock over this sudden death. I don't recall how my mother and sister-in-law made the funeral arrangements. I don't know how my sister-in-law and her children or our family made it through such grievous time.

Eventually, my sister-in-law and her children later moved back to Oglethorpe where they built their house.

House on the red clay, 1965

We lived in Andersonville on Freedman Hill. Later, my mother sold her house and bought some property beside the main highway 49, the only highway to get to Oglethorpe and Americus. We lived in a four-room wooden house; the bedrooms were pretty large—two regular beds could fit in each room. In the center of this house was a two-sided fireplace (a two-sided fireplace is one fireplace faces roof). The largest bedroom was in this area; this was where we slept and where neighbors congregated, talked, and prayed. The house had two front wooden doors and two back wooden doors. I believe there were two sets of windows to each room and two sets in the front *(draw a pic of the house with the windows)* and two in the back, with a tin roof, no electrical wiring attached, no bathrooms, and no plumbing pipes. I don't recall my mother packing any household items. Looking back, I'm sure she wrapped her dishes and things that could be broken.

Moving the house was something any child would have stood in awe and watched. Seeing a four-bedroom house loaded onto a long, wide-load trailer truck with flags waving and moved to the property several miles away was a feeling of lost. On the other hand, I did not like that location because it was red and very muddy in front of the house when it rained. At the back of the house was a long wooded alley way, with weeds, hedges, vines trees, and who knew what else—it was very scary at times, and not many houses near ours. Although I did not like the property, it was not for me to question my mother who worked so hard and wanted the best for her children.

Teenage tornado

In early 1965, at approximately fifteen years of age, I experienced one of the most traumatic times in my life. My mother allowed me to stay at a family member's house. While staying there, I was abducted and forced into a car (against my will) by two guys. Despite my crying, screaming, and kicking, trying to stop them, they were much stronger, so they overpowered me. Sad to say, another person sat on the porch and saw these young adults (the driver of the car was her brother) force me into their car but did absolutely nothing to stop them or even attempted to prevent what is known today as a serious crime. They squeezed me into the front seat between them both and drove away to a house that seemed to be not far from where I was visiting. The driver parked the car in a very dark, shaded area away from the house, got out of the car, and went into the house for a while, leaving me alone and allowing the perpetrator ample time for him to rape me.

Sometime later, the driver returned to the car to find me, the little girl from Andersonville, frightened and crying hysterically. Of course, I was confused and in shock, trying to fathom what had just happened to me. Before I could blink, they speed off, driving me back to the house from which I was abducted. Before putting me out of the car and driving away, their facial expressions displayed "mission accomplished." Where do I go from here? The individual was still sitting on the porch watching as I was put out of the car. Her first words were "You better hope you're not pregnant." I wondered if she was in on the scheme! It was somewhat late. There was no telephone, no school counselors, no neighbors, and no police, and I didn't know what to do, had no one to share this difficult moment with me, and just did not know how to tell my sister-in-law with whom I was staying what her brother and his friend had done. I recalled not sleeping well for days, nervous and in shock. I cannot explain the fear and mental anguish I endured for years.

Very scared and confused

Several days later, I returned home to Andersonville, where I began re-living this nightmare. I really cannot explain how I was feeling in my body. During those times, I can honestly say it was indeed not a good feeling. I felt defeated, betrayed, helpless, and being taken advantage of at the same time. Of course, no longer a virgin, I was unable to focus mentally, and I felt used and emotionally confused. I started to develop a low self-esteem and could not tell my mother what had transpired for fear of further repercussion—I was so depressed. I even lost interest going back to school.

The way out

In late 1965, in pursuit of finding a better job and educational opportunities, my sister Doris and I rode down to Miami, with cousins who were returning from Andersonville to Miami, at the time. We came to live with our oldest brother and his family who were already living in Miami. In reality, moving to Miami, things began to feel much better, right from the beginning. In fact, it was a very good "way out"! Months later, mother and the younger three siblings, along with my nephew and niece, finally moved to Miami, where we all resided, together as one big, happy family.

At age sixteen, I had no idea which direction I should take in life to escape the hidden pain I experienced inside. I no longer had an interest in school; however, I knew I had to make a change. Searching for answers, I don't believe I was afraid to tell. I just didn't know how or who to tell. At times, I gave little or no thought to the incident.

Mental, emotional, and physical labor

Reluctantly, I accepted a job ironing clothes a few blocks away from where we were living. The family also owned a barbershop. When payday came, the wife sent me to the barbershop to collect my pay, which I did! For five days' work, from a.m. to p.m., he paid me less than $20. Well, that was the end of that job! I felt cheated, sad, and humiliated. This was another emotional blow for me. I was already hurting, feeling rejected and worthless, and still mentally and emotionally buried under the tornado that recurs from time to time.

As I continue to deal with my inner tornado, I just could not find the courage to tell my mother what had happened to me. Still reluctant to return to school, I continued looking for work. My next job was cleaning people's homes and working in hotels and motels. After more than a year, I soon realized that this was not the kind of work I wanted to do. I knew I needed to make a change and do better and not allow the hidden tornado to hinder me from accomplishing my life's goal.

Life-changing break

In late 1966, I was referred by an employment agency to Job Corp to take a cashier training in Clinton, Iowa, which I attended for approximately ten months. Even though I was very far way and missed my family, I could not get rid of the internal tornado that continued to haunt me. I was still not able to tell anyone or know how to ask for counseling. Along with myself, there were two or three other African-American girls at the training. A few of us girls would go places at times when some nice guys would come along and ask us out—and no, the "little girl from Andersonville" had no boyfriend there. I was too scared, and we girls were all too young to enter the nightclubs. Another disadvantage, it was predominantly a white town. Furthermore, the weather was not too friendly either. It was very cold and snowed during the months we were there. Not having very much to do, we had no television, cell phones, or computers; we mostly stayed in our dorms or sat around socializing with one another.

Upon completion of my training in late-1967, I returned to Miami where I lived with my mother and several other family members in a one bedroom apartment, in the 934 Village at 6805 NW 7th Court.

Excited about my new career, later that year, at age eighteen, I started my first real job as a cashier at A & G Grocery Store. My starting salary was $1.65 per hour. One night as customers checked out through my line, a man came through with a double-barrel shotgun pointed at my face and said some words in a low-tone voice; not aware I was being robbed, another cashier said to me, "Give him the money. Give him the money," and I did, praise God for protecting me.

CHAPTER 4

How did I get the name "Rose"?

While working at this store, something wonderful happened to me that would shape my life for the future—I met this very handsome, neatly built young black man with curly hair and pearly white teeth. I was the cashier; he was the bagboy. He asked me, "What is your name sweet thing?"

I replied, "Rhodessia!" After many times trying to pronounce my name, he gave up and started calling me Rose. That is how I got the name Rose.

We courted for a while and soon fell in love. Months later, we began dating. Later, I rented an apartment at 7001 NW 15th Avenue. At age nineteen, I became pregnant. It was a very difficult pregnancy for me. I could no longer work, so I moved back to live with my mother, this time, in a two-bedroom apartment at 6809 NW 10th Court. Without hesitation, my fiancé assumed the responsibility caring for me.

Sunshine

At age twenty, on Monday, September 8, 1969, at 10:44 p.m., our baby arrived. I gave birth to a gorgeous baby girl, weighing in at seven pounds. During my pregnancy, I craved for Argo starch—please do not try this at all! I ate so of that stuff, our daughter was born with Argo starch in her hair!!! Approximately five days later, my child and I were discharged from the hospital and were picked up by my fiancé. So excited to be new parents, we did something really silly. We left the hospital and went straight to the Grand Way Department Store on NW 54th Street and 12th Avenue to buy clothes for the baby. Warning! Once again, please do not leave the hospital and go straight to the store with your newborn baby—very risky!!!

The cloudy scare

Approximately three weeks after our daughter was born, on September 30, 1969, my fiancé was drafted into the U.S. Navy. As a result, he had very little time to spend with us, as he prepared for leaving. On that fateful day, I do not recall if the recruiter drove him to the airport or he took a taxicab. Whatever mode it was, all three of us, along with the driver, rode together to the airport on the day of his departure. Not only was this a scary moment for us, it was also one of the most devastating days of my life. Despite all the hugs, kisses, tears, and promises, saying goodbye was so uncertain, as the love of my life was leaving for war, and he may never return. This was a tough pill to swallow. As I watched the sad look on his face, trying to fight back tears, we could not find words to express our love and feelings for each other.

The closer it got to waiting to board the plane, the more emotional we became. With our daughter in my arms, we kissed and said our last goodbyes as he boarded the plane and waved. I became more emotional. A million thoughts went through my head. Here I am, a young, immature mother with a new baby to care for on my own. It was indeed the hardest decision we both had to make, not knowing if we would ever see each other again, and his two-weeks-old daughter would have to grow up without her dad in her life.

On our way home from the airport, I cuddled my baby daughter tightly in my arms and took the bus. Once on the bus, I kept staring outside the window. With tears streaming down my checks, I silently prayed that we would see each other again. I took the bus to downtown Miami and transferred to another bus on N.W. 7th Avenue and 68th Street. It was night when we arrived home. Thank God for his protection. Still hugging my daughter, I kept gazing out the window in total shock. It was a long ride from Miami International Airport to the village where my mother lived.

Despite the scare and fears, there was a ray of hope in me knowing how to trust and depend on God. Deep down inside, I was just clinging to some knowledge of God which I gained from going to church with my mother as a little girl in Andersonville. Several weeks after my fiancé was stationed, he wrote us a letter—what a relief that was!!! Reading his letter had somehow strengthened my faith. I was instantly motivated and would no longer allow fear to block my destiny. Approximately eight weeks later, I landed another cashier's job, this time at a department store. Shortly thereafter, I had saved up enough money to get an apartment. I would push my daughter in a stroller each morning for my mother to babysit and pick her up after work.

Months later, I got a job as a cashier at K-Mart Department Store in Hialeah to support my daughter and myself. I moved into a one-bedroom apartment on 62nd Street and 12th Avenue. There was no stove, refrigerator, or furniture. I had an old regular-size used bed. It was not easy getting up early in the morning walking and pushing the baby ten blocks to my mother to babysit her in the mornings and picking her up late evenings.

I moved to another one-bedroom apartment at 1281 NW 61st Street, Apartment #31, the same building where my younger sister lived. I bought a sofa, a dresser, a heavy iron table with four chairs, an old stove with only a few burners working, and an old refrigerator from a thrift store in Miami.

I later lost my job at K-Mart due to misunderstandings with the head cashier. I later got a job at Lucky's Market on 62nd Street and NW 22nd Avenue, working in the meat department. I couldn't bear working in a very cold place. I despised looking at dead cows and pigs hanging in the freezer and the grounding and cutting of meat. The trimmings from the meat was raked into a large black barrel, later used for ground beef. The job didn't last too long. I began receiving state assistance.

With little state assistance, I enrolled in a program which was funded by the government. I took clerical classes, which I didn't really care for. I had no one to really guide me to what may have been the best career for me.

The Unexpected Navy Visit

In 1970, approximately, a year later, one fateful day, I had got off work and picked up my daughter, and as we arrived at the apartment building, I looked up and surprisingly saw this handsome young man dressed in his navy white uniform, resting on the rail of my the third-floor apartment, looking down, anxiously awaiting for us to arrive.

Dumbfounded, overjoyed, I instantly lost my nerves. I was so excited, and at the same time, I panicked. So overwhelmed, I asked my neighbor to let me come into her apartment to check myself to make sure I looked okay. She, too, was excited for me; she did not hesitate to let me come in (thanks, Ms. Shirley). After gaining some composure, I picked up my daughter on my left arm, baby bag on the right shoulder, the little folding stroller in my right hand, and up the stairs I went. What a happy reunion this was! I was so flabbergasted—our "prince charming" had returned. After spending several glorious days with us, he returned to the navy. Once again, the nervousness, tears, and some fears—not as much as before—resumed. However, this time, it was a different feeling altogether. I was somewhat more matured. I quickly came to the realization that I did not want to live a sinful life anymore. Still unaware of what was taking place, I must have just turned my life over in surrender to God almighty, because at the time, I had no one to really confide in, and with whom I could express my feelings as to what I was really dealing with. There were those who went to church and professed holiness but never told me about Christ. Reflecting back on the unexpected visit and the uncomfortableness, it was God dealing with me.

CHAPTER 5

A Mighty Rushing Wind

For John truly baptized with water;
but ye shall be baptized with the Holy
Ghost not many days hence.

—Acts 1:5 (KJV)

On this fateful Friday night in 1971, approximately between 8:00 p.m. and 11:00 p.m., I was somewhat relaxed and listening to a gospel album entitled "*Prayer 1971 (Vinyl LP)*," *by* Rev. Ruben Willingham. As I recalled, I was sitting on a sofa chair (covered with a pink chenille bedspread) with my daughter lying on my lap. As the music serenaded my spirit, I found myself worshipping and thanking God, not really understanding or even realizing what was taking place in my life at that moment. I was starving inside; I didn't understand I was spiritually hungry. Matthew 5:6

(GW) says, "Blessed are those who hunger and thirst for God's approval. They will be satisfied."

> When Pentecost, the fiftieth day after Passover, came, all the believers were together in one place. Suddenly, a sound like a violently blowing wind came from the sky and filled the whole house where they were staying.
>
> Tongues that looked like fire appeared to them. The tongues arranged themselves so that one came to rest on each believer.
>
> All the believers were filled with the Holy Spirit and began to speak in other languages as the Spirit gave them the ability to speak. (Acts 2:1–4, GW)

As I sing along with the music, I began to weep bitterly. I was just praising and thanking God aloud. Suddenly, I recalled speaking in a strange language (similar to the one my mother experienced years ago). Still naïve, at the time I was not aware of what was happening to me. All I knew, it was an awesome experience and the most beautiful time in my life. I will never forget that fateful night at 1231 NW 61st Street at Apartment #31 in Miami, Florida, when God saved, sanctified, and filled me with the Holy Ghost. All I knew, it was a glorious experience that I could never forget. It made me feel different, clean, and light-hearted. I just felt God's peace, love, and joy hovering over me.

After my encounter with God, I looked through the little glass peephole window in the door and saw neighbors standing on the porch in front of my apartment. Later that night, I went to sit on my porch. There, I came face to face with my neighbors who were also standing on their porches. They seemingly heard me praising God and speaking in a strange language. I did not know how to explain my experience to them—I was still in amazement as to what had just happened to me spiritually, mentally, emotionally, and joyfully. Little did I know that this was the beginning of my brand new life. At the time, I didn't know the Lord was drawing me closer to him. In my heart, I wanted to be a good example for my daughter. I attended church faithfully and joined the "Atchison's Specials," which was a singing group. As I dedicated myself to singing, the Lord dealt with me in a much stronger way. My life took on a new meaning.

I remember, as a child, when *my mother* took me to church, one Sunday morning, during one of the elder's sermons—I recalled several of his sermons—he said, "You must be born again; none shall see him but the pure in heart!" Although I was too young to fully comprehend what those words meant at the time, they resonated in my heart, and I always remembered them in my spirit.

The Supernatural Power of the Almighty God

As my desire increased to go to church, days later, I walked into my neighborhood drugstore at 54th Street and NW 12th Avenue where I stumbled upon and bought a little Bible for approximately $3.00. As I meditated on the words in the scriptures from this little Bible, my life began to change significantly—I wanted more than everything else to be baptized in water.

Matthew 5:6 (KJV) says, "Blessed *are* they which do hunger and thirst after righteousness: for they shall be filled."

I was spiritually hungry; not knowing naturally how to seek, however, God knew what I was in need of at that moment. I believe; this was the supernatural intervention of the spirit of God.

And it came to pass, that, while Apollos was at Corinth, Paul having passed through the upper coasts came to Ephesus: and finding certain disciples.

He said unto them, "Have ye received the Holy Ghost since ye believed?" And they said unto him, "We have not so much as heard whether there be any Holy Ghost."

And he said unto them, "Unto what then were ye baptized?" And they said, "Unto John's baptism."

Then said Paul, "John verily baptized with the baptism of repentance, saying unto the people, that they should believe on him which should come after him, that is, on Christ Jesus." When they heard *this*, they were baptized in the name of the Lord Jesus.

And when Paul had laid *his* hands upon them, the Holy Ghost came on them; and they spoke with tongues, and prophesied. (Acts 19:1–6, KJV)

Paul knew how important it is for believers to be filled with the Holy Spirit after they confess the Lord Jesus as savior.

I am so happy God saved me in my apartment alone; no one can get the glory but God! Hallelujah! Hallelujah!

Now That I Believed

Fully convinced, I knew I no longer wanted to live in sin. I was baptized months later but became very disappointed when I learned that there was no night service after their baptism. This was an experience I pray I will never forget. I did not want to go home. I attended church faithfully; I even became a member of the "Atchison's Specials" singing group. The Lord dealt with me in a much stronger way. My life took on a new meaning. Shortly thereafter, I joined Mt. Calvary Missionary Baptist Church where I received water baptism on a Sunday night. After baptism, I sat on the first pew. However, I became somewhat disappointed because there were no night services there either. Still, from that day onward, my life has never been the same.

Mentally, emotionally, and joyfully, this was the beginning of my new life. I started attending the Mount Calvary Missionary Baptist Church which was only a block away from where I lived. After baptism, I became a member of the church, as well as singing with the "Atchison Special Choir." When I had to go to choir rehearsals, I would take my daughter with me and seat her on the front pew. I would give her something to read—maybe a page from the newspaper. At two years of age, she would sit quietly and read her paper upside down. I attended faithfully rehearsals and Sunday services. When the Atchison Special Choir was invited out to sing, I was willing to go; however, I had to take my baby girl with me. I took my daughter everywhere with me, except work. I did not want to impose on my mother or anyone else to care for my daughter while I attend rehearsals. Due to my hunger and thirst for righteousness, I was glad to be involved in the choir. This helped me in my new life.

Statement of Faith

I am a secure believer in the Holy Bible and believes in the following.

It is the inspired scriptures. All the Scripture (Old and New Testaments) is divinely inspired of God and is the only authority of faith and godly conduct (II Tim. 3:15–17).

God. Only one true and living God, all things were created by him. God is all-knowing. He is eternal love, the redeemer of mankind. He reveals himself as the Father, Son, and Holy Ghost (John 1:1–14).

The Trinity. Scripturally, we may speak almighty of the God of heaven as a trinity. He is one Lord. God has revealed himself in three distinct personal attributes and yet absolutely unified into one (John 1:1–14).

Deity, our Lord and Savior Jesus Christ. God's Word explicitly declares:

- Jesus' virgin birth—Matthew 1:23
- Jesus' sinless life—Hebrew 7:26
- Jesus' substitutionary sacrifice on the cross—1 Corinthians 15:3

- Jesus' bodily resurrection from the dead—Matthew 28:6 and 1 Corinthians 15:4
- Jesus' is seated at the right hand of the Father—Acts 2:33

The fall of man. God created man good and free of any evil. Man of his own will transgress the will and command of God, thereby inheriting the nature of sin which results in physical death as well as spiritual death apart from God the Father.

The salvation of man. Man can only be redeemed by the shed blood of Jesus the Son of the living God. This salvation is received through repentance toward God and faith in Jesus Christ, being justified by grace through (Romans 10:9–15).

The inward witnesses of the Spirit and the outward witness of a holy and righteous life are the evidences of salvation (Romans 8:16; Ephesians 4:24).

Water baptism. Baptism of water by immersion is commanded in the scriptures. Baptism symbolizes that the person has died with Christ and has been raised with him in newness of life (Matthew 28:19; Romans 6:4).

The Lord's supper consisting of bread and the fruit of the vine expresses our sharing of the divine nature of the Lord (2 Peter 1:4). All believers should share in this memorial the Lord's supper until he returns. As we partake in the (Lord's supper) holy communion, we must remember his suffering and death (1 Corinthians 11:26).

The infilling with the Holy Ghost (Holy Spirit). This being the normal experience of all in the early Christian church should be experienced by all in the body of Christ. With the infilling with the Holy Spirit comes a deeper reverence for God and fullness of the spirit, endowment of power in our life and service, and a greater love for the things of God (John 7:37–39; Acts 2:42; Acts 2:43; Acts 8:12–17; 1 Corinthians 12:1–31).

Speaking in other tongues. The physical sign of speaking in tongues is Bible evidence of the baptism of believers with the Holy Ghost (Acts 2:4; 1 Corinthians 12: 4–10 and 12:28).

Communion/the Lord's supper.

And as they were eating, Jesus took bread, and blessed *it*, and broke *it*, and gave *it* to the disciples, and said, "Take, eat; this is my body." (Matthew 26:26–29, KJV)

And when he had given thanks, he broke *it*, and said, "Take, eat; this is my body, which is broken for you: this do in remembrance of me."

After the same manner also *he took* the cup, when he had supped, saying, "This cup is the new testament in my blood: this do ye, as oft as ye drink *it*, in remembrance of me.

For as often as ye eat this bread, and drink this cup, ye do shew the Lord's death till he come." (1 Corinthians 11:24–26, KJV)

Sanctification. Sanctification is the act of being set apart from evil and sin and the lusts of the world. Identifying with Christ and faith in his sacrificial death and resurrection, the believer's sanctification becomes a reality to him (Galatians 2:20; Hebrews 12:14).

The body of the Lord Jesus. Jesus Christ is the head of the church, his body, and is its source of authority and power.

Each person who has been born of the spirit is an important part of the body of Christ. The minister's divine mission command of the Lord Jesus Christ is to take the gospel to all the world and to make disciples of all nations (Matthew 28:19–20; Ephesians 1:22; Hebrews 12:23). This ministry is established to evangelize the world, worship God, and edify the body of saints (Mark 16:15–20) and help bring change to family members, neighborhood community, city, state, and around the world (John 4:23–24; Ephesians 4:11–16).

Gifts of the Spirit: Divine healing and miracles. Perfect health is provided for in the atonement and is the privilege of all believers. Divine healing and miracles are a part of the gospel of Jesus Christ (Matthew 8:16–17; James 5:14–16).

The resurrection. Those dead in Christ will rise first, and then those who are alive and remain shall be caught up together with them and so shall we ever be with the Lord. This is the precious hope of the church (1 Thessalonians 4:16–17).

The millennial. This is the time when Christ will visibly come back with his saints to reign on the earth for a thousand years. There will be universal peace at this time (Isaiah 11:6–9; Zechariah 14:5; Revelations 20:1–6).

The judgment. Whosoever's name is not found written in the lamb's Book of Life shall go to everlasting punishment and torment; while the righteous shall enter into everlasting life and peace (Revelations 19:20).

The Scare

My daughter was about two and a half years old, and she and one of our little neighbors around the same age were playing on the third floor of the apartment building we lived in. However, as some mother's do, while the children are playing, we involved ourselves in cleaning, cooking, or conversations with our neighbor. Whatever I was doing, reflecting back on that scare as a young mother living on my own, I went to the door to check on the children. As I look at my little daughter sitting between the rails with the back backward, all I could do was scream and run and grab her before she leaned back, thank God he bangles. He helped me check on her just in time. Had I not had checked on her, she would have felt backwards from the third floor to the pavement down below. But thank God for watching over my daughter. However, I continue going to church and working and also took up clerical courses at Lindsey, a Hopkins. My life continued improving daily.

Joy in the Midst of a Storm

On August 4, 1971, my fiancé was discharged from the United States Navy. I did not know how to explain my transformation to him and what had happened to me. Pregnant the second time, I felt very strange inside, this was not right; nor was it pleasing in the sight of God. Not knowing at that time what the bible says concerning fornication. I shared this feeling with my fiancé. We must get married or separate. He agreed that we get married. We had one child and another on the way; we were in love with each other and knew marriage was God's way. The blessed and right thing to do was to get married.

> Now concerning the things whereof ye wrote unto me: It is good for a man not to touch a woman. Nevertheless, *to avoid* fornication, let every man have his own wife, and let every woman have her own husband. (1 Corinthians 7:1–2)

With the good news of marriage, I spoke with my pastor who agreed to join us together in holy matrimony. We were married in a very humble ceremony on Saturday, March 11, 1972, in the afternoon, at Apartment #31, 1281 NW 61st Street, Miami, Florida, by the late Reverend Samuel Atchison. My dress consisted of a navy blue maternity skirt, light blue top, and black shoes. The groom was casual. We had two little flower girls, no flowers and no rings, just Gods' approval. The blood tests were $10.00, minister's fee $10.00, and marriage license $5.00. The total cost of our wedding was $25.00, in 1972. After the ceremony, the four of us went to the children's hospital to visit my husband's little nephew who was very sick. This was one of the happiest days of my life.

CHAPTER 6

Family Shockwave—
Tragedy Strikes Again

It was mid-December, 1971—I was pregnant—when I received the very heartbreaking news that my third oldest brother had been shot and killed. I was told that the security guard at A & P Supermarket on NW 62nd Street was responsible. Family members were asked to go to the mortuary and identify the body. One of my younger brothers Joe went to identify the body. Several days later, my older brother's girlfriend, and I went to view the body at the House of Albert Funeral Home in Miami on NW 15th Avenue. His funeral service was held at the church I attended. At this stage, it is painful losing a brother whom I had gotten close to and suddenly now he's gone. Only God knew what my mother and the rest of the family was going through. We had no thought of seeking counseling or support groups. My mother had to depend on God to get her and the family through this time of grief and difficulties.

As a result of the death of my brother, the grief, and my pregnancy, I had dropped out of the program and decided to stay home until the baby was born. Newly married, new Christian, my husband in college, and working is a cross no pregnant mother or anyone would choose to bear. Not knowing the promises of God, my faith and trust was in him. Psalm 12:6 (GW) says, "The promises of the *Lord* are pure, like silver refined in a furnace and purified seven times."

Bundle of Joy in the Midst of Pain

Early Friday morning, May 25, 1972, I went into labor. My husband took me to Jackson Memorial Hospital. While waiting in the labor room distressed with labor pain, the contractions increased rapidly. I screamed out, "Nurse, call the doctor the baby is coming!"

They just checked and said, "Not yet," and left the room. Finally, after all the pain, at 5:48 p.m., I gave birth to a handsome baby boy.

Several months later, the doctors diagnosed our son with spinal meningitis. Neither my husband nor I knew what spinal meningitis was or how serious it even was. Consequently, our son was hospitalized at Jackson Memorial for several weeks. When we would visit our baby, it was extremely painful, as we were not allowed to pick him up or hug him. We surrounded his little bed, hoping for a miracle. As his mother, seeing so many tubes and/or wires hanging from his tiny little body; needles in his arms, hands, feet, and forehead; and machines beeping around his bed was very devastating for me. Suddenly, it made me realize that this was really serious.

Whenever I would go to visit my baby, walking into that room and seeing him lying there in the same position was very devastating for me. At the time, I was a new Christian, and I didn't know anything about spiritual warfare, praying in the spirit, or even calling someone else to pray with me. Ironically though, deep down inside I could feel, not sure at the time, but reflecting back it was my spirit man rising up in me and making intercessions for my baby. My husband and I did not realize it, but in the meantime, I believed in God and that my baby would live and not die. That was my faith in action as a new Christian. Praise be to our Lord God almighty, he heard and answered my prayers. Our son was healed, and days later he was discharged from the hospital. Praise the Lord. God had a plan for my son's life. What the enemy meant for evil, God turned it around and worked it out for good—praise the Lord!

New Start! New Home!

In August 1973, we moved into a brand new townhouse, located at 3402 Carol City, Florida—this was a predominantly all-white community. The two-bedroom townhouse consisted of two baths, a stove, a refrigerator, and a washer/dryer. We purchased new furniture, carpeting, a new floor model, and a *colored television. Also, this was the year* I received my driver's license, and my husband bought me a new dark blue 1973 Nova car; he drove a Volkswagen. We were all so excited over this new transition. My husband was also elated just finishing college and *landing* a new job.

As I share my story, it brings tears of joy looking back on the goodness of God and how faithful he is to his promises. We, as believers in Christ, should often take an inventory of our lives, calculating the goodness and faithfulness of God. In so doing, it will cause us to fall in love with Him all over again.

Shattered Hope

So excited over what God had blessed us with, my growth in God was unexplainable. I was seeking a church that I could attend closer in the area. One day I passed by a nice church just blocks from where we lived. Now, excited, hungry for more of God, I got the kids ready and put them in the car and off we went. I was not aware that it was an all-white church. However, as I drove to the gate, the parking attendant at the gate immediately started waving his hand telling me, "No, you cannot come here." You cannot imagine what I felt at that moment—the shock and the disappointment after all the anticipation and the planning, my little children too young to understand my hurt.

Holding back the tears, I turned around and left, not sure if I ever told my husband. See, as a babe in Christ, I did not see a black or white salvation. I remember in the natural, when my daughter and son were born, as their mother, they were too young to recognize race, gender, or even where their food was coming from. Their desire as a baby was "change me, help me, and feed me", likewise the encounter that I had with God—my desire, my thirst, and my cry were fed. After all, the almighty God says in his word:

> So I get rid of every kind of evil, every kind of deception, hypocrisy, jealousy, and every kind of slander. Desire God's pure word as newborn babies desire milk. Then you will grow in your salvation.
>
> Certainly you have tasted that the Lord is good! You are coming to Christ, the living stone who was rejected by humans but was chosen as precious by God. You come to him as living stones, a spiritual house that is being built into a holy priesthood. So offer spiritual sacrifices that God accepts through Jesus Christ. (1 Peter 2:1–5, GW)

I had enough of the old life. I am a new creation in Christ Jesus. I was changed. Undoubtful, I had tasted that the Lord was oh so, so good! I would not have traded this life for anything else. Although my old life was not a bad one, according to Psalm 51:5 (GW), "David said, 'Indeed, I was born guilty. I was a sinner when my mother conceived me.'"

I realized I was born in sin and shaped in iniquity. I no longer wanted the past lifestyle. This new life is surely what every soul should long for—to be reconciled back with his/her creator, our Heavenly Father. Thank God, I did not allow that one—the enemy—to take away or stop God's plan for my life.

*****

Still very hungry for the things of God, one Sunday the kids and I were on our way home from the church where I attended at the beginning of my new birth in Christ. We passed a little white church called Triumph the Church and Kingdom of God on NW 22nd Avenue. My heart craved for fellowship with God and with others who knew him. I said to myself, "I will go there next Sunday!"

The following Sunday, I got the kids ready, put them in the car, and off we went. Not knowing what to expect, I was excited but a little nervous—the thoughts of what had happened at the other church; yet I persevered the more. My kids and I went inside, very small Pentecostal congregation, maybe five to eight older people—I did not recall seeing any children in the service. However, the number of people there was no major concern for me. I was hungry for God.

After the minister ended his sermon, he opened the doors of the church for membership. To the altar I went. I was so excited. I joined their church that very same day and rededicated my life to the Lord. At the end of the service, the kids and I returned home joyfully. I was excited about what had happened. I told my husband I had joined the church. He seemed a little disappointed but did not stop me from attending the services. I attended services faithfully for about one year. I finally realized they did not serve communion nor did they offer water baptism. When I asked one of the mothers of the church, she stated the reason they did not baptize or serve communion, she replied, "The Lord told the bishop to stay away from water." I asked, sarcastically, if the bishop go fishing a lot, she replied yes! So the bishop assumed the Lord was saying for him to stop the ordinances. I was deeply concerned about the ordinance during my time there.

*****

I had suffered from kidney stones; the doctor wanted to do surgery. After the doctor showed my husband and me the X-rays with three kidney stones, I did not stay in the hospital; I put my faith in God! Instead, I fasted and prayed for several days. The saints also prayed for me, again. And, you know the answer, the kidney stones passed. Praise the Lord. In gratitude, faithfully, I began seeking God's guidance.

I was diagnosed with severe migraine headaches, so severe I could barely perform neither motherly nor wifely duties. In the meantime, my husband was in college, working and would come home and help with the children and other duties. After suffering so long, the medication was not helping. As a child of God and my faith grew stronger, I called the saints/elders from the church that I was attending; they came over to my house. We agreed on the Word of God and in prayer, trusting God to heal me. That night I was healed and delivered, from migraine headaches. Praise God!

The Prayer of Faith and Scripture Healing

If any of you are having trouble, pray. If you are happy, sing psalms.

If you are sick, call for the church leaders. Have them pray for you and anoint you with olive oil in the name of the Lord.

(Prayers offered in faith will save those who are sick, and the Lord will cure them.) If you have sinned, you will be forgiven.

So admit your sins to each other, and pray for each other so that you will be healed. Prayers offered by those who have God's approval are effective.

Elijah was human like us. Yet, when he prayed that it wouldn't rain, no rain fell on the ground for three-and-a-half years.

Then he prayed again. It rained, and the ground produced crops. (James 5:13–18, GW)

First Near-Death Experience: It was not my time to slip into Eternity

On December 7, 1973, at the age of twenty-four, the doctors diagnosed me as having chronic pelvic inflammatory infection. I was admitted into the hospital for an operation. The doctors had explained the procedure to me slightly before which gave some assurance that everything would be alright. After preparation for the operation, the next thing I felt was someone slapping my face yelling, "Mrs. Strong, wake up, wake up." I don't recall responding.

It seemed that I was far away. However, the next day I woke up, and there were tubes, heart monitors, flashing lights, and intravenous (IV) tubes in my hand and arms which appeared to be covering my body. Meanwhile, the doctors and nurses were standing at the foot and side of my bed in amazement, looking but saying little of what had happened. I was under the impression that was the way it was after one had surgery.

Later, the patient in the bed next to me rose up in the bed looking and smiling saying, "They called code blue on you last night. Doctors and nurses were trying to revive you."

That evening my husband came to visit me. Lying in bed facing the door, I saw my husband passing the door slightly looking into the room. The look on his face was that of awe. He backed up and came into the room. Praise God, I was discharged several days later.

Looking back on that near-death experience, it was not my time to slip into eternity. With a very loving husband and two small children, God had another plan for my life.

A Second Near-death Experience

On October 15, 1974, I was admitted to the JMH hospital with an ovarian cyst. Immediate surgery was needed, according to the doctors. Again, the enemy tried to destroy me, but God delivered me. There were other challenges that I encountered, but, thank God, I had a loving husband who was there every step of the way. While pursuing his education and working, he took the time to care for the kids and as well as being a caregiver for several months. He displayed the vows we made the day we were married—*for better or for worst!* Great is his reward in heaven.

*****

I remembered my third oldest sister becoming very ill and was hospitalized for quite some time. When I would visit her, she could hardly talk; she looked as though she was in despair and always seemed worried about her children. It was painful observing her fragile body, weighing less than 100 lbs., and hooked up to machines, heart monitors, and feeding tubes. Nevertheless, in my heart, I desired to see my sister healed and out of that hospital. Not knowing the Lord as I knew him later, I began to pray and lay hands on her. Days later, she started eating on her own; she began to gain weight and was discharged from the hospital. How can I forget those memorable moments with my sister? God almighty restored her back to health.

*****

In 1976, my husband encouraged me to go to college. Right then and there, I realized that in order for me to better myself in this society and in the job market, I would need a college education, hence, my enrollment in fashion design classes at Miami Dade Community College. Unfortunately, the instructor was a prejudice and a selfish person who hardly ever had encouraging words for the students. While attending college, I developed a different outlook on life. I learned that education was a powerful tool and a very pivotal component in one's life. So off I went in pursuit of education.

In May 1978, I graduated with an associate of science degree in fashion design. Shortly thereafter, I landed a job working for a pattern-making company in Miami. While working there, I applied for substitute teaching with Dade County public schools. Frankly, I was told by personnel in the county that I would not be able to start substituting by the time school started. In my quest to succeed, I did not take "no" for an answer; instead, I went straight to the throne of God. Ironically, by the time the school year rolled around, my paperwork was completed. Praise God! As a result, my name was added to the substitute teachers' list. In addition, I also earned a post to substitute regularly at American Senior High School where my husband had previously worked.

*****

What was once considered a nice, quiet neighborhood suddenly started changing into a low-income housing community. As a result, families began to move to other subdivisions. With new families moving in, noise and traffic control started to get out of hand. Hence, we, too, had to move out of the area.

Moving for us was certainly a move of faith. So we went off in search to find our new home. My husband, kids, and I set out on a path looking mostly in an all-white neighborhood—we were excited about the beautiful homes and quiet, well-kept community. As we drove slowly on different streets, admiring the beauty of a serene neighborhood, suddenly we heard gunshots rang out at our car. We also had similar experiences with congregants in all-white churches. Hence, we did what anyone in their right mind would do—we speeded out as fast as we could and vowed not to return. From there, we went on to another development which was also very beautiful. Once we indicated an interest to purchase, we were told that availability of this community would not be ready for over a year. Not sure if they even told us the truth. We kept looking at other new developments but had our heart set on this particular one that we really liked and wanted.

My husband had recently got a permanent teaching position in a school a little ways away from our home. Although we did not have much income, we were somewhat in a good place. Our young son was now in daycare, our oldest daughter in elementary school. Another thing we had going for us was excellent credit. My husband felt we would be eligible to qualify for a bank loan—were we ever in for a rude awakening! Every time my husband would check on the status, they would give him a negative report to decline. After being rejected several times by the bank, as a believer in Christ, I decided to put my faith in action. So one day I left work, drove down and parked in the driveway of an unfinished house which the builders were working on, got out of my car, and declared these words, according to Joshua 1:3 (KJV), "Every place that the sole of your foot shall tread upon, that have I given unto you, as I said unto Moses." I walked around that property seven times, repeating, "This is my house"—not worrying what people thought of me then—that house was ours, I claimed it and received by faith, in Jesus' name.

Well, by now, you've guessed the answer! Several weeks later, we received a small piece of paper—*not a nice letter in the mail*—that read: "You've been approved." Upon receiving the news, I held my two kids by their hands and started dancing, praising, and thanking God for the manifestation. When my husband came home from work, I gave him the note. As a business teacher with knowledge in home buying, he immediately understood the qualification process. After my husband read and digested the note, he was flabbergasted at what God had done. He was convinced that this was God's doing. This was a move of faith that drew him closer to God. In a very short time, thereafter, with God's favor, we all moved into a brand-new home, in a clean, quiet neighborhood, with phenomenal neighbors. This is a proven fact that *with faith in God, all things are possible when we believe.*

Manifestations of Blessings

Later, I was hired to fill a teacher assistant position which became available at a middle school in the special education department. A study position was also available for a teacher assistant in the special education department at Hialeah Middle School. In both capacities, I interacted with and learned the art of dealing with students who were having emotional difficulties. This was a great challenge for me.

I recalled, one day, during my prayer and Bible study time, not knowing what the future holds, the Lord gave me these words in Psalms 118:17 (GW): "I will not die, but I will live and tell what the Lord has done."

A Third Near-death Experience: Less than six hours to live!

During the early hours of the morning of February 8, 1983, I was awakened by an excruciating abdominal pain which came on suddenly. All I could do for relief was press my hands hard into my stomach, fold my knees in a ball over my hands, and cry, "Jesus!!!" The pain was so severe; all I could do was keep calling on the name of Jesus. My husband called the doctor on duty for the night and was instructed to bring me into the office at 9:00 a.m. the next morning. For the remaining hours, I remained in the bed, tossing and rocking from side to side, too weak to walk around, just wishing for daybreak. This was a long night, indeed.

Finally, it was the next morning and time for me to go see the doctor. Still riddled with pain, I lay in the back seat of our blue Cordoba, over and over pressing my hands into my stomach and making a ball with my knees in my hands. As my husband drove by one of our neighborhood schools, I began vomiting some brownish/greenish bitter fluid. My husband pulled the car to the side of the road, allowing me to hang my head outside the window. I was so weak; I could barely pull my head up to lean forward behind the front passenger seat. I pulled my head back into the car then off my husband drove.

Upon arrival at the doctor's office, I was checked in immediately. Minutes later, several doctors examined me, taking X-rays and asking questions—some of which I was too weak to comprehend and answer coherently. Vaguely, falling in and out of sleep from grogginess, I could hear them discussing among themselves—"Something is wrong. Something is there." They could not discern the problem very clearly from the X-ray to make a decision. I could hear them trying to make a decision as to what to do. The office made arrangements for me to be admitted to the hospital at 2:00 p.m. In the meantime, I was discharged and sent home to wait for appointment time. Home again, waiting and wishing for the time to return to the hospital, it was like eternity. Again, I was pressing my hands in my stomach, crying, grunting, and calling on the name of Jesus to ease the pain. The pain was so excruciating, I felt as if my eyes were getting larger, and I was far, far away.

Finally, it was time to go to the hospital. The pain had intensified. Upon admission at the hospital, staff quickly wheeled me into a room—presumably the X-ray department—I would say it was the X-ray room because I acknowledged the clicking sound of the machine. The pain was so excruciating, still crying and grunting, I could hardly see the doctor who was standing so close to my bed. I even heard him asking questions which I was unable to answer, based on the severity of my pain. Because of the pain, I was incapable of answering questions accurately. I recalled saying, "Doctor, please just let me go to heaven."

I could hear the doctors conferring, "We must operate right away. What do you want me to do?"

I also heard my husband responding to the doctors' question, giving a "yes" by saying, "Go ahead, doctor, operate."

The doctor gave me less than six hours to live if I didn't have the surgery. As a result, emergency surgery was performed for a small bowel obstruction. Later that night, I was still drowsy with a heart monitor and an IV in my arm and a tube through my nose to drain the remaining poisonous fluid from my stomach. I woke up in a room with dim lights. My husband and other family members were standing around my bed with very sorrowful looks on their faces but thankful that I was alive.

Softly stroking my hand, my husband candidly said, "We thought we had lost you," with a smirk (smile) of relief on his face. All glory be to God, I knew I had, once again, conquered death.

The next morning, the doctor came into my room with a joyful look on his face. He asked, "How do you feel?"

I replied, "Alright" or "Fine"—not quite sure what I said. He began explaining to me what was wrong. To help me understand what had happened, he pulled out a white handkerchief from his pocket holding one corner in his right hand and another corner in his left hand. He began twisting the handkerchief so tight until it began to knot up.

He said, "This is how your small bowel had backed up in your stomach, causing everything to turn into gangrene, thus, causing a death and decay of bodily tissue." It was only then that I realized how seriously ill I was. I had no idea how long I had the small intestinal blockage, but I know it was not an overnight situation. I later realized, God knew what was going to happen on February 8. He gave me his word: "I will not die, but I will live and tell what the *Lord* has done."

After more than seventeen days' stay in the hospital, I had a devastating conversation with one of my visitors. Frankly, this was something very upsetting that interfered not only with my healing but also with my sleep. The entire night I tossed, prayed, cried, searched through the scriptures, and sought for an answer. This conversation caused a setback that resulted in my stay at the hospital for several days more. Oh, but my God kept me!

Hence, I remained in the hospital for approximately eighteen days, prior to discharge. At all times, one should be very mindful of what they say to others. Before you ask what happened, pray! Before you start a conversation, pray! Before you pray for the patient, pray! Before you start criticizing, pray! Before you start prophesying to the patient what you feel he or she should do, pray! I recall the old axiom: "Sticks and stones may break my bones, but words will never hurt." I found out saying the wrong words can vex a persons' soul especially at the wrong time.

A soft answer turneth away wrath: but *grievous words* stir up anger.

The tongue of the wise useth knowledge aright: but the mouth of fools poureth out foolishness. (Proverbs 15:1–2, KJV)

Thank God for his grace and mercy.

CHAPTER 7

A New Place of Worship

During this time, my children and I were attending a traditional fellowship; however, the ministry was going through a transitional period. I was very hungry for the things of God. I knew I had to seek another place to worship. One Sunday, the kids and I were visiting an in-law church. On our way, I noticed a sign on a school ground with service times of another church.

Several Sundays later, my husband took the kids to a tournament. As I stood at my kitchen sink, cleaning chicken to prepare dinner, the Holy Spirit spoke to me and said, "This would be a good day to visit this new church at the school." Immediately, I stopped, put the food in the refrigerator, and got dressed and off I went. I visited and enjoyed the worship. It was a small group of people, less than fifteen, but the worship was awesome. Thereafter, the kids and I continued attending the services. As the congregation grew, the ministry rented a storefront and started having weekly services. On July 3, I became a member. I volunteered to work at the church for several weeks to help get the church situated and served wherever I could.

Female Minister

On June 24, 1984, I became the first licensed female minister to preach the gospel in the ministry where I, my husband, and kids served for many years. Although I faced many challenges, I did not quit. Instead I was more determined to serve the *Lord*.

On January 23–25, 1986, I conducted a powerful revival meeting sponsored by Rose of Sharon Ministries, Inc., Miami, Florida. I was not quite certain what God had in store for me at the time. However, I do recall him impressing upon my heart to design and display a banner during the meeting, with the names and definitions of "God." Unknown to us, at the time, there was a Jewish event happening right next door to our service. When the people heard us worshipping God, many of them came over and celebrated with us as we sang worship songs—including some Jewish songs!!! What an awesome meeting that was. The Lord had done great things at that meeting—a meeting that stood out significantly in my mind, a memory I have always cherished, time after time.

Standing in the Gap

I *recalled standing* in the gap for my husband for several years, *praying that he would* give his life back to the Lord. My husband was a real dedicated family man, a loving and caring husband, and a great father. According to God's Word in 1 Corinthians 7:13–14, "If any Christian woman is married to a man who is an unbeliever, and he is willing to live with her, she should not divorce her husband. Actually, the unbelieving husband is made holy because of his wife, and an unbelieving wife is made holy because of her husband. Otherwise, their children would be unacceptable (to God), but now they are acceptable to him."

In Mark 11:22–24 (GW), Jesus said to them, "Have faith in God! I can guarantee this truth: This is what will be done for someone who doesn't doubt but believes what he says will happen. He can say to this mountain, 'Be uprooted and thrown into the sea,' and it will be done for him. That's why I tell you to *have faith that you have already received whatever you pray for, and it will be yours.*"

When other believers would hear me openly confessing that my husband was saved by faith, I was expecting the supernatural manifestation of what God says in his Word. However, when others doubted, I continued confessing and believing what the Word of God says. I believe I spoke and acted on it according to God's Word. Thank you, Lord, my husband is saved by faith. I'm only waiting for the outer manifestation.

Acts 16:30–31 (KJV) says, "And brought them out and said, 'Sirs, what must I do to be saved?' And they said, 'Believe on the Lord Jesus Christ, and thou shalt be saved, and thy house'" (my husband).

In April 1987, as I accompanied my husband down the aisle to the altar on that Sunday morning, my dear husband gave his life to the Lord. I had never seen nor heard such noises of praise and rejoicing when someone gave their life to the Lord. I could visualize what was happening in heaven. Luke 15:10 (KJV) says, "Likewise, I say unto you, there is joy in the presence of the angels of God over one sinner that repenteth."

He joined the ministry on July 5, 1987. Along with our two children, we both served faithfully *together* in that ministry for many years.

> This is the testimony: God has given us eternal life, and this life is found in his Son. The person who has the Son has this life. The person who doesn't have the Son of God doesn't have this life.
>
> I've written this to those who believe in the Son of God so that they will know that they have eternal life. We are confident that God listens to us if *we ask for anything* that has his approval.
>
> We know that he listens to our requests. *So we (I) know that we (I) already have what we ask him for.* (1 John 5:11–15, GW)

August 1987, I started substitute teaching two to three days a week. In addition, I opened and operated a little boutique called *Simple Clothing*. I worked in the afternoons, renting tuxedos and making bridal and prom gowns, dresses, alterations, and invitations. My husband thought that it was too much for me and that I didn't have to keep the shop. I closed the shop and moved the business into my home where I worked at my own pace.

Servant Hood 1988-1989

> "And whatsoever ye do, do it heartily, as to
> the Lord, and not unto men;"

> Colossians 3:23 KJV

God has called all of us believers to serve in his kingdom in this earth. However, we must do whatever we can from the heart, not expecting money, fame, or a pat on the shoulder for everything we do. We must remember, we serve God in our home/family, on our jobs, in ministry and in our community. We must respect our leaders, our supervisors, etc., but not worship them; we are to give all the praise, all the glory and all that honor onto our Lord God Almighty. God is going to reward us for our labor.

1990–1995

In August 1990, I was offered a job with the ministry we were attending; it was a non-profit ministry. After discussing it with my husband and much prayer and fasting, I accepted the job. This was the most challenging decision I ever had to make regarding employment. I could foresee that it was going to be very problematic working there because of the anointing on my life and my stance for holiness. From the very first day I went to fill out the paperwork, the test began. It was not easy being a licensed female minister at that time. I was determined that I would not allow anything to interfere with the plan of God in my life.

I was constantly reminded of Psalms 34:19 (KJV): "Many are the afflictions of the righteous, but the Lord delivers him out of them all." During my employment with this ministry, I began to realize that this was the plan of God for a season. However, I understood God's special plan for my life and that this was a time of servanthood and training for future ministries. I would not give up. I did not quit! Why should I? In Matthew 5:10–12 (GW), Jesus said:

> Blessed are those who are persecuted for doing what God approves of. The kingdom of heaven belongs to them. Blessed are you when people insult you, persecute you, lie, and say all kinds of evil things about you because of me. Rejoice and be glad because you have a great reward in heaven! The prophets who lived before you were persecuted in these ways.

I thank God for the tests, the trials, and the persecutions that he allowed me to encounter. I became spiritually stronger, bolder, and more determined to win souls for the kingdom of God.

Prophecies and a Word of Knowledge from the Lord

August 23, 1992, after the 7:00 p.m. service, the night of Hurricane Andrew, the Lord spoke these words through one of our guest speakers during the conference. "God is preparing you for ministering—you are a leader! God has taken you as far as he can at this point. Something great within the next five years will happen. You won't change (meaning I will not compromise, I will continue to stand for holiness and righteousness). God is going to send people—people are drawn to you. I see sheep around you. You will be traveling. It is a great work. There will be changes— one thing then another, example, prayer ministry for a season, then something else, etc."

Now there was no way I was going to tell anyone this part of the prophecy as the guest minister prophesied to me about the ministering. I kind of pushed it to the side. I thought within myself, *God is not going to call me to minister.* As time passed, I found myself not thinking of ministering, saying, "Lord, it is not my desire to be a minister. I have nothing against women ministers but not me! God, you will really, really have to speak to me—minister, *um, um me?*" I can hardly minister myself. I have seen what some ministers have to deal with. I know I can't be a minister.

God gave me a study on the "fivefold." As I did the study, it was my desire to please God and to preach the gospel of the Lord Jesus Christ. At the time, I was not aware that epistles of first and second Timothy were ministerial epistles. During the time of study, my spirit would bear witness with the Word of God depositing in my spirit—a minister's heart. In the midst of what God was doing in my life at this time, a family storm hit. However, that did not stop the plan of God in my life. The enemy did not get the victory. Amen!!!

CHAPTER 8

The School of Wisdom, Staff Trip to Washington DC

March 3–9, 1993

Something Special

As I prepared for the trip, I could feel in my spirit that something good was going to happen in my life—something special!!! And, without a doubt, this was the best staff trip ever. God had deposited something inside of me that I could not explain. For starters, I met some very delightful people—some of whom were business owners and others were ministers of the gospel. As we communicated, it began to feel like we were old friends—the fellowship was so divine!!!

Some members of our staff were invited to join the bishop and his wife in their suite for an evening of fellowship. When we arrived, I was in awe to be in the presence of this renowned Nigerian bishop and his wife. I had no idea I was going to meet these wonderful people face-to-face, but, seemingly, the Lord had already planned it. My husband along with two other couples rode together in the van to different events. We had lots of fun and fellowship. The first night of the Ministers Conference School of Wisdom, before the Bishop ministered, his first statement was: "Before you sit, I want you to know this year is a different year in your life. Sometimes you need someone to remind you of what God told you to do."

Special Talents

Dorcas Fashions, specialized in African *attire/*accessories, consisted of tuxedos, bridal wear, and specially made garments. Fashion and talent shows *were another hallmark creation implemented to encourage* children and youth in public schools, churches, and other special events, motivating them on the importance of building low self-esteem and demonstrating their talents constructively through fashion, arts, music, and much more.

CHAPTER 9

Basking In His Presence

Speak, Lord, Your Servant Is Listening

It was Sunday morning, July 31, 1994, basking in his presence, I decided to go sit by the pool and study the Word of God. I wanted to sit by the side of the pool and just put my feet in the water. So I sat at a table on the southwest side of the pool, while others swam or sat and talked to one with the other. The Spirit led me to the book of Titus. I opened my Bible and began to study and meditate on the Word of God. God's love began to unfold like ripples of living water. I could feel the spirit, the heart of Paul's instructions to Titus, and how he was to set things in order and ordain elders, according to their qualifications for elders, leaders, etc.

As I continued studying, my spirit was totally in agreement with the Word. However, I had to stop; it was time for us to check out of the hotel. After we checked out, we toured a resort. During the tour, God's constant reminder would come up in my spirit. Even though I would be thinking and responding to my husband as we looked out on the beautiful land, homes, and very peaceful scenery, simultaneously, the Word of God continued popping up in my spirit on how Titus was to teach the people in Crete. It was so awesome how my husband and I were speaking at the same time when the Word of God was bubbling inside my spirit.

On the other hand, it is a great and urgent need in the body of Christ for people to know for sure that God almighty has called them to "the fivefold ministry." There are many ways that God calls Christians.

> He also gave apostles, prophets, missionaries, as well as pastors and teachers as gifts (to his church).
>
> Their purpose is to prepare God's people, to serve, and to build up the body of Christ.
>
> This is to continue until all of us are united in our faith and in our knowledge about God's Son, until we become mature, until we measure up to Christ, who is the standard.
>
> Then we will no longer be little children, tossed and carried about by all kinds of teachings that change like the wind. We will no longer be influenced by people who use cunning and clever strategies to lead us astray.

Instead, as we lovingly speak the truth, we will grow up completely in our relationship to Christ, who is the head. He makes the whole body fit together and unites it through the support of every joint. As each and every part does its job, he makes the body grow so that it builds itself up in love. (Ephesians 4:11–16, GW)

Learn what this means: "I want mercy, not sacrifices." I've come to call sinners, not people who think they have God's approval. (Matthew 9:13, GW)

God didn't call us to be sexually immoral but to be holy. God calls us all unto holiness. (1 Thessalonians 4:7, GW)

There are many other scriptures that talks about "call, called, and calling" but not pertaining to the fivefold ministry call. Many people have and will make the mistake of thinking God has or is calling them into the fivefold ministry. It is true that a child of God is called to minister—minister means to serve. We are all servants of the most high God.

God's call is to mercy, not to sacrifice. What God wants first of all is a person's life. God wants to cleanse the person and make him acceptable for heaven. Once God has the person's life, he has all he is. Some postpone the call of God, and some deny the call of God; they close their minds entirely.

A great need for laborers, we as believers need to answer the call to laboring in our communities, city, neighborhoods, etc.

> Then he said to his disciples, "The harvest is large, but the workers are few.
> So ask the Lord who gives this harvest to send workers to harvest his crops." (Matthew 9:37–38)

Here is another great *call*—prayer. Laborers are needed 24/7, 365 days, to pray. Nonetheless, how many believers truly accept this call? We so quickly yield to the fivefold ministry gifts. But they must be the laborers of God, for the harvest is God's. It is entirely *inadequate* by any means to handpick the laborers and send them forth; this will not get the work done alone. God's call and his appointment are vital. Jesus is saying, "Pray that *God* will rise up plenty laborers to reach the lost, the hurting, and the broken in our generation and the forthcoming generations. As this day and age believers, it is our responsible to answer the call to pray!"

As I talked to my father, asking him what he wanted me to eat scripturally at that time, he gave me 1 Kings 19. I read verses 11–21, which anointed and saturated my spirit, however, verse really resonated in my spirit. Elijah found Elisha plowing (working) with twelve yolks of oxen before him. Elijah passed by him and casted (put his mantle upon him). I believe that the mantle were so stunning, so awesome, Elisha left the oxen and ran after Elijah and said, "Let me go kiss and say goodbye to my father and mother, then I will go with you."

Elijah said, "Go, what have I done to you?" Elisha returned, killed and roasted the oxen, and gave it to the people to eat. This was a celebration of Elisha's promotion. So Elisha left his people and followed Elijah in ministry.

Excited about God's Word, I returned to reading the book of Titus, eager to hear what God was saying to me. I could feel that God was revealing something.

As I walked into the lobby at church, the lights were out. I walked down the aisle toward the front of the sanctuary to sit down—praise and worship was just about to begin. A strange feeling started looming over me. Although it was hot, the feeling was not totally the feeling from the heat. I did not quite pick up what was happening spiritually. At times, the minister would confirm what the Lord already placed in my spirit. Many times in intercessory prayer, God will speak to us through his Scripture/Word or through a word of knowledge.

As the ministers made their way to the platform, I thought to myself, *What was going on other than the lights being out?* The minister preached a very short message, and as he was coming to the conclusion, I left to attend to after-service duties. I *heard* the minister speaking to the congregation, as was his norm after altar call. I distinctly heard my name, so I assumed that minister was encouraging the people to come out to prayer on Saturday. I continued with my duties as I heard these words from the congregation: praise God, Amen, glory, etc. As I looked up, I made eye contact with a sister in the Lord. The smile on her face indicated that something good had happened. I asked her, "What happened? What did he say?"

She replied, "Assistant minister."

I said, "Who?"

She said, "You!"

I said, "No, Minister didn't say that!"

She said, "Yes, he did!"

Then I heard others in the lobby say, "Assistant minister!" To see the expression of happiness on some faces assured me that this was God's plan for my life in this season.

The Call of God

He also gave apostles, prophets, missionaries,
as well as ministers and teachers as gift (to His
church)." Their purpose is to prepare God's people
to serve and to build up the body of Christ.

—Ephesian 4:11–12 (GW)

Before God calls you into the fivefold ministry, he will equip and train you for the area in which you are called. You have no experience, little knowledge of scriptures, and no understanding of church structure or legal ramifications. (I know nothing is too difficult for God; however, God ordained government.) When difficulties occur, you don't know who to ask for help. Your marriage is dysfunctional, but you haven't given God the chance to cleanse you, but you say, "I know God called me to minister." Maybe the word minister did pop up in your spirit, your heart, or your mind. You see, when one becomes born again, you are a baby Christian. The Word of God calls us sheep—John 10:6—every sheep needs a shepherd (minister).

You need to be spiritually equipped. Think for a minute—would you send a child across a busy highway? No! No one in their right mind would do such thing. Now, if you tell a person eighteen years or older who is capable of making his or her own decision, do not walk across I-95, they would say, "I know how to get across. I'm old enough. Don't tell me how to cross." After you warn them of the danger and the tragedy and they don't listen, what more can you do? As the fivefold ministry gifts, our purpose is to prepare God's people to serve and to build up the body of Christ.

There Are Many Warnings in God's Word

> Do your best to present yourself to God as a "tried-and-true worker who isn't ashamed to teach the word of truth correctly." (2 Timothy 2:15, GW)

> Every passage is inspired by God. All of them are useful for teaching, pointing out errors, correcting people, and training them for a life that has God's approval. They equip God's servants so that they are completely prepared to do good things. (2 Timothy 3:16–17, GW)

When God calls you, he will equip you for that area of ministry. Remember, if you call yourself, if you allow man or the devil to call you, you will end up feeling confused and wounded, because you rushed and missed the voice of the almighty God.

If God calls you to do something, believe that he will manifest it in his time. He will have everything in order. Now, there will be trials, persecution, and afflictions, but you'll be able to say like Paul and Timothy, "What persecution I endured: but out of them all, the Lord delivered me." Why? As 2 Timothy 1:11 says, "Because the Lord God almighty had called, appointed him a preacher and an apostle, a leader of Gentiles." When he suffered, he was not ashamed. Paul knew whom he believed and was persuaded that he was able to keep that which was committed unto him against that day—"What day?" The day and time of persecution and affliction. During that time, you will be able to stand and hold fast the form of sound words which you have heard in faith and love which is in Christ Jesus. That good thing which was committed unto you is kept by the Holy Ghost which *dwells* in us (2 Timothy 1:13–14, AMP).

*****

On December 11, 1994, I was ordained as an assistant pastor of the Prayer Ministry. At that time, I really had to be strong mentally, spiritually, and emotionally. The warfare, the tests, and the trials I encountered, from many who claimed to have known Christ, had increased. However, I had more victory than defeat. God gave me the strength to withstand through them all.

A Time to Unclutter

To everything there is a season, and a time
to every purpose under the heaven.

—Ecclesiastes 3:1 (KJV)

In our lives, we clutter a lot of unnecessary items in our home, on our job, in the office, especially us ladies— shoes, clothes, purses, etc. Let's not leave out the men and even children who have learned to clutter at an early age. I raise my hand. I'm guilty of stuff I know I do not need but won't let go. I confess, I still have my first garment I designed for a fashion show. On the other hand, as I have gotten older, I don't care to keep things I don't need. Is this how it is? We come to realize it is time to let go of the weights that we have. Since we are surrounded by so many examples (of faith), we must *get rid of everything that slows us down,* especially sin that distracts us. We must run the race that lies ahead of us and never give up. Too much clutter can confuse us, hinders our progress, and can cause us to lose focus on God's purpose for our lives.

August 1995 was a very difficult time in my life. My husband and I went to a conference, hoping that we would be able to really hear from God. Nevertheless, the emotional pain, the pressure of ministry, and the fiery darts seemed to have uprooted some childhood issues. On the other hand,

I thought I was getting rest physically, but how can one really rest physically when their mind is constantly in competition thousands of miles backward—in our childhood? Despite the odds, I knew I had to get away and really seek God concerning what was happening inside of me. Having such a loving and caring husband and although he knew some of what I was going through as the assistant minister, after I was ordained he, too, was able to discern that something was not right. We were very close and open with each other; he allowed me to express what I was encountering. As I began telling him about the events in 1965, he immediately put his arms around me, holding and assuring me that he loved me regardless of any mistreatment from others. He empowered me to open up and vent and break free from the presence of past childhood traumas that haunted me. At the end of the conference, my husband and I knew it was time to get away and really seek God in a time of prayer and fasting. I'm not sure how I got the information about the conference to be held in Atlanta, Georgia, in September. However, it was God-ordained.

CHAPTER 10

The Unforgettable Trip to Atlanta, Georgia

Seven Days of Seeking God

In September, 1995, I went to a meeting in Atlanta, Georgia. During our time of fasting, praying, and seeking God, I had an impartation of some awesome things—that changed my life for the better. My mind was renewed, the *joy* of my salvation had been restored, and clearer directions were received from the Lord concerning his will for my life.

I had gone as far as I thought I could spiritually, mentally, and physically. It seemed as if I was at the end of my rope. Stressed out with pain all over my body, I could barely hold my head up because of the pain. When we arrived at the hotel and after checking in, the first room to me was unbelievable. I called the desk and we took a look at another room, not knowing they were giving us a suite for the same price. The suite was not much better; we were told they had nothing else available until Tuesday. We took the suite, overlooking the room, in the hope of transferring to the promised suite on Tuesday. We kept looking over the room, complaining about the drapes, the carpet, and the smell in the bathroom. I knew I could not eat in this room. However, the Lord convicted me that we should stay in this room.

Later, I told my roommate how the Lord revealed for us to stay in this room. She agreed. As I began to concentrate on the size of the room and small amenities, the Spirit showed me there will be times when I will have to stay in places much worse. I thought about what was happening, repented, and began to thank God for small mercies. In reality, we thought, where would we get a suite for $70 a day—nowhere! After thinking positively, I was able to eat and drink comfortably. After all that was said and done, I thanked God for my deliverance. Never again will I complain; I thought about Jesus who had no bed, no house, etc. In my spirit, I knew that God wanted me to take this trip. I humbled myself and needed to clean up my act prior to returning to Miami.

As I continued receiving confirmation from the Lord, so many times on things concerning the things that were in my spirit, I knew that I had to get to a place where nothing or no one could distract me—no phone, no job, no husband, or no housework. My main goal was to focus on God and seek his will for my life. When we got to the service, the banner hanging over the platform read, "'Seeking God for seven days' Jeremiah 29:11–13." My spirit rejoiced; it was comforting to have that agreement in my spirit. Instantly, I began thinking about the number eight—new beginnings. My roommate and I had shared suite number 1801. I went to Bible reference to see what the Word of God says about the number eight—it means new beginnings.

The prophetess who hosted the meeting stated that she sought the face of God which will help her to have this meeting in September, which is the fruit of the womb, the birthing month. Again, my spirit rejoiced. I began thinking about my purpose for attending the conference. I knew in my heart that I needed to give birth spiritually. I was irritated, with pains in my body, and no appetite. To think of it, this is the way it is in natural labor for one with a child.

The Night of Expectancy

As we arrived at the church, people were very, very hungry for what God was about to do. The spirit of expectation was present all around the room. The people worshipped and praised God with the highest enthusiasm. There were two speakers; they set the atmosphere for us to receive what God had in store for us for the next seven days. The second speaker preached the Word of God. The Spirit of God moved nightly in the midst of his people. One of the speakers, seemingly in her late seventies or early eighties, with a special anointing, began laying hands on the people. In the isle near where I was sitting, I looked over to my right, and all I could see was my roommate's right leg elevated, and people were falling everywhere, under the power of God. The transformation of the Spirit of God's anointing was heavy upon her as she ministered to the people. As this speaker went down the aisle, it was not the usual way. I began moving under the power of the Holy

Ghost. I had never been in a meeting where only Jesus was lifted up in pure holiness; people were falling and crying out to God—his presence was truly in this place. When we left at approximately 11:49 p.m. that night, people were still on their faces seeking God.

The next day we arrived at the church, people were sitting, some were on their knees, and others were reading the Word of God, as everyone waited for another move of the Spirit. Personally, I was sitting meditating and thinking on the goodness of God and what he has revealed to me at the meeting. I began confessing to God how much I loved him and how much I wanted his will to be done in my life. With tears in my eyes, I looked at the banner over the platform that said, "Seeking God." This truly bore witness to my spirit, and that was the real reason I came to the meeting—seeking God! As a woman in love with God, I knew I had to have a change in my life—I wanted more. We sat and waited on God to have his way in us. As the speaker made her way to the platform, a roaring praise erupted to God. A sister and I went to the altar, as the power of God went forth in a very mighty way—a time of new beginnings.

Waiting Upon God

> Lead me in your truth and teach me because you are God, my savior. I wait all day long for you. (Psalms 25:5, GW)

Wait with hope for the Lord. Be strong, and let your heart be courageous. Yes, wait with hope for the Lord. (Psalms 27:14, GW) Wait calmly for God alone, my soul, because my hope comes from him. (Psalms 62:5, GW)

I will wait for the Lord, who hides his face from the descendants of Jacob. I will hope in him. (Isaiah 8:17, GW)

It's another night—waiting penitently for the move of God. People continued seeking God by reading the Word, staying on their knees, looking around with anticipation, and sitting in the quietness of the Holy Spirit, as we all reverenced God in this place, adults and children alike. One could not help but feel the presence of the Lord. It was so sweet, worshipping, meditating, and falling prostrate at the feet of Jesus. Service began with praise and worship, followed by prayer of warfare which broke out in the service. Everyone began praying corporately and fighting in the spirit. People were just walking to and fro and speaking the Word of God, denouncing spiritual wickedness in high places, and pulling down strongholds.

The Word of God was mighty and powerful throughout the service. According to Romans 12:1–2 (GW) brothers and sisters, in view of all we have just shared about God's compassion, I encourage you to offer your bodies as living sacrifices, dedicated to God and pleasing to him. This kind of worship is appropriate for you. Don't become like the people of this world. Instead, change the way you think. Then you will always be able to determine what God really wants—what is good, pleasing, and perfect.

> But first, be concerned about his kingdom and what has his approval. Then all these things will be provided for you. (Matthew 6:33, GW)

Instead of seeking material things—things with less value, which are not eternal—seek God who is the giver of these things. Don't seek healing—seek the healer. Don't seek ministry—seek God, the giver of ministry. Seek God; he is the one that gives you the power to get wealth. Don't seek blessings—seek the blesser. God is the one that will supply all your needs. We are to seek the things that are in God's kingdom.

September is defined as birthing month. This makes me realize that I had to release something old and birth something new in my spirituality. Therefore, this trip was geared toward seeking God and his will for my life—letting go of the old and embracing the new.

CHAPTER 11

Do Not Reject the Voice of God

But seek ye first the kingdom of God, and
his righteousness; and all these things shall
be added unto you. (Matthew 6:33, KJV)

In October 1995, the Lord began to really deal with me about resigning from my job as an assistant pastor and starting a radio broadcast ministry. I began to seek God to be sure I was in his perfect and divine will. This was a very sensitive issue. All things must be done decently and in order, so I shared with my husband what God was dealing with me about resigning from my job, not knowing what was ahead. After our discussion, my husband gave his approval. I called together approximately twenty-one people whom God had placed in my spirit, and I shared what God had instructed me to do. They all came in agreement and prayed with me. Much prayer was made for this transition. In the meantime, I continued working in the origination. Thank God I obeyed his voice.

My Love's Fiftieth Birthday
Celebration December 1995

There is difference *also* between a wife and a virgin.
The unmarried woman careth for the things of the
Lord, that she may be holy both in body and in
spirit: but she that is married careth for the things
of the world, how she may please *her* husband.

—1 Corinthians 7:34 (KJV)

Looking forward to having a surprise fiftieth birthday party for my husband, although my husband was not a fan of having birthday parties, I wanted to do something very special for his fiftieth birthday, just to show my appreciation and adoration for him. It turned out to be an awesome party, indeed, and most of all the food was delicious. As each guest arrived with gifts, cards, and lots of smiles, he was filled with surprises, all of which were evident in his smile and the expressions of joy on his face. In the end, he was very happy that the children, myself, and family members gave him such a memorable fiftieth birthday celebration.

Radio Outreach to the Community

On January 1, 1996, Morning Revival Ministries launched its very first broadcast. The topic was "God has a plan and purpose for our lives," taken from Ezekiel 26:25–27. Morning Revival Ministries was an outreach ministry (not a church building) committed to restoring the family structure and to help bring change to our neighborhoods, communities, and cities. Morning Revival Ministries endeavored to reach the "total man" through prayer and the Word of God. The ministry's main goal was to bring deliverance and hope to those who are abused and plagued by the effects of drugs, crime, alcohol, oppression, depression, and sickness.

February 1996, God dealt with me again! This time, it was concerning resigning from my job as staff assistant minister. Since I am a people person, I enjoyed serving others, witnessing and hearing their testimonies. Although I wanted to continue, I wrestled with resigning for a while. Sitting at my desk, days later, working on prayer assignments, I heard in my spirit the voice of God very strong. "Resign or suffer the consequences." Well, you know that did it for me! God did not have to tell me a third time.

Again, I talked it over with my husband. Financially we were good, so he had no problem with me resigning. After much praying and fasting to make sure it would be a smooth transition, I met the CEO and vice CEO of the ministry concerning resigning. I also told them about the vision the Lord had placed upon my heart concerning outreach radio ministry.

In March 15, 1996, I resigned as staff assistant minister. After my resignation, the CEO expressed to me that on the 17th there would be an ordination service in the evening. Ironically, I was the first to be commissioned out by the minister in that ministry. Hence, I became a full-time minister of Morning Revival Ministries, Inc.

First Ladies' Prayer Retreat

On November 21, 1996, Morning Revival Ministries sponsored a two-day prayer retreat in Bradenton, Florida. Oh, what an awesome time we had with God! Spiritual healing, deliverance, salvation, and much more happened during that prayer retreat.

Helpless, Hopeless, and Homeless

I remember, it was a Saturday afternoon, when I received a telephone call that my third oldest sister was being evicted from the place where she was living, after the death of her husband. The landlord explained what was taking place. I did not hesitate. I shared the problem with my husband. He was moved with compassion and encouraged me to go and help her. When I arrived at the apartment seeing my sister's condition, I knew God had to intervene, and he did, in my sister's favor. I watched God changed her life in the process of chaos.

The Family Reunited

Months later, still not knowing of her children's whereabouts was silently weighing heavily on her heart. The mental, emotional, and physical pain that had been embedded for many years appeared to have pushed her into a state of depression. After carefully observing the condition she was in, I was motivated to search for her children's whereabouts. I don't recall how God did it, but he did it. I was able to locate all of her children but one. Although they were already young adults, they were reunited with her. I am so grateful to God. It was not easy, but because of God, my sister is saved today. This brought so much joy to her, our mother, me, and other family members. Read more about my sister's life story. "My Sister, My Friend" Amazon.com

CHAPTER 12

Cherishing a Dear Mother

Mother's Whirlwind

In December 1996, I received a report from the doctor that my mother had a brain tumor and was given approximately three months to live. He further advised that she needed round-the-clock care. I knew I had some decisions to make. It was either that I placed her in a nursing home or have her live with my husband and me in our home. I also knew the day would come when mother would need extra special care. I consulted with her doctor who had advised me initially. The doctor assured me that there was no need for surgery at her age. Worst-case scenario, she could be placed into the hospice care program. I talked with my loving husband, and he agreed to allow mother to live in our home.

Mother's Happiness

Children, obey your parents because you are
Christians. This is the right thing to do.
Honor your father and *mother* that everything may go
well for you, and you may have a long life on earth.
This is an important commandment with a promise.

—Ephesians 6:1–3 (GW)

On January 6, 1997, we moved mother into our home;
hence, the task begun. The first couple of months, mother
was able to walk around and do some things on her own,
with minimal supervision. My sister-in-law and I would
take mother out to the mall, to lunch, sightseeing, and
visiting. After an enjoyable day of fun and fellowship, we
would return home, and I would help mother get prepared
for a good night's sleep.

The month of March was very special—it was mother's birthday month. I planned to give her a birthday dinner, but it seemed almost impossible to get all the family
together. Eventually, eight of us took her to dinner. Mother
seemed somewhat disappointed or, perhaps, she was not
feeling her best. Several months later, I began to notice that
mother's physical and mental health was slowly declining.
However, her spiritual commitment remained steadfast.
She continued to lift up the name of Jesus with daily praise
and thanksgiving. At times I would quietly sneak into her
room, and she would be resting peacefully. Other times, I
would stand at the door and just look in to make sure she

was still breathing. The Lord revealed to me in dreams and visions that mother was preparing for her home in heaven. She craved for special foods. Thank God, we were able to provide for her every need. It was evident that mother enjoyed the last eight months of her life immensely.

Getting Ready for Her Heavenly Home

Monday, August 11, 1997 God showed me in a vision that it would not be long before mother leaves this earth for her heavenly home. The nurses and assistants were always overwhelmed to see how strong mother was physically and spiritually. Patients with her kind of illness, they would recall, were usually in severe pain and very weak. When I realized how ill mother was, my request was, "Please God, do not let her suffer." I had seen people in the hospital with the same illness, screaming and crying for someone to help them, but there was no one to help ease their pain— not even pain medication. I knew it would really affect me mentally to see my mother suffer that way.

Tuesday, August 12, I was led to stay home from Bible study and make mother's home-going attire and gather other family information.

Wednesday, August 13, mother had no appetite; she just wanted to rest. She had gotten very weak; her last steps were between 10:00 a.m. and 11:00 a.m. I sat by her bed-side, pinning hankies together to be sewed. Holding her hand and talking with her as she lay in bed, I asked her, "mother are you getting ready for heaven?"

Grabbing the cover on the bed and pulling herself up, she said, "Yes! I'm going to see Jesus!"

I asked her, "Are you going to leave me?"

Again, she said, "Yes! I'm going to see Jesus, honey."

There was so much joy in her expression and peace on her face as she lay in bed looking upward as if she had seen angels or something glorious/heavenly. That night I was, again, led by the spirit of God to call her nurse to come and check mother. She was not in any pain. However, upon the nurse's recommendation, other family members assisted me in getting mother ready for admission to the hospital. Today is August 14. It was evident that it would not be much longer before mother went home to be with the Lord. I called some of her church members to visit mother in the hospital, sing songs, and pray with her. The members visited her, and this brought much joy and encouragement to her heart. At a glance, one could see that mother knew she was getting closer to her heavenly home.

On August 16 between 7:10 a.m. and 7:15 a.m., the Lord gave me a vision concerning mother. The telephone rang and woke me out of the vision the Lord was revealing to me. Ironically, it was the nurse from the hospital. Calmly, I asked, "What's wrong?"

The nurse said in a soft voice, "She's gone! She didn't give us any indication that she was leaving."

I told the nurse, "Mother was not supposed to give an indication." I had asked God to allow her to go peacefully. I started to cry. I knew that I would miss her, but I was thankful to God for not allowing her to suffer. God granted all of my requests concerning mother. Upon receiving the news, I called the family and asked them to meet me at the hospital. When I walked in the door where she lay, my mother was facing the east with such a peaceful look on her face. I knew she was in heaven.

August 23, 1997, what a joy it was to know that mother was absent from the body and present with the Lord. She was resting from all her labor. What a celebration! What a time of rejoicing, praising God for eighty-six years, five months, and twelve days of life. Mother is in heaven now, but many precious memories remain. I will cherish them! The experience gained from caring for my mother has had a lasting impact on my life. I realized that there comes a time in all our lives when we will need someone to help in difficult times. Caring for my mother gave me the joy to grow old. However, to be able to care for yourself when you get older is a greater joy. Christians have the responsibility to care for those who cannot care for themselves. When our time comes, we will definitely reap the good we have sowed.

There were times when I felt that I could not do for mother what I had to do for her. I did things I never thought or dreamed I would do. But with God, my husband, daughter, brother, sister-in-law, and the assistance of others, mother was able to live a comfortable life. The last eight months were the best times of her life. It is extremely important that Christian families face reality that this world is not our home. We are here for a period of time. People prepare for weddings, graduations, birthdays, etc., but most people shy away from the issue of mortality. We must use discretion and prepare ahead for such a time as losing a love one. We need to be prepared mentally, spiritually, and financially. By doing this, it truly relieves the family from a lot of stress. Thank God I had prepared ahead of time.

In 1998, after the death of mother, my involvement in the ministry and encouragement from my husband inspired me to continue my education, hence my enrollment in interpersonal group communications studies at Trinity International University.

CHAPTER 13

A "Wave" Is coming, A Wave
of the "Holy Ghost"

On May 27, 1998, during the 11:00 p.m. phone prayer, the Lord spoke these words: "A wave is coming, a wave of the Holy Ghost." As I continued to meditate, I asked God what he meant by wave is coming. During my prayer and study time on June 2, between 1:20 a.m. and 2:25 a.m. the Lord began to reveal this wave to me.

This wave, no man can stop it. It is a move of my spirit. In this wave, people will be forced out by my spirit to do the work of Christ. This wave is so powerful, they will not be forced out against their will. Some will feel they may be moving too fast, and some will feel they must have lots of money, but because they desire in their heart and spirit, they will be persuaded by my spirit to go and do the works of Christ Jesus.

This wave will be a mass movement. In this wave, there will be different things, a special force that will cause my people to go back and forth, up and down, proclaiming the gospel. God is going to transmit his anointing by his spirit into his people. The anointing will cause them to go from one place to another place. This wave is going to be a great impact, very forceful, and very effective. Man won't be able to impress people. The influence will be by my spirit. In this wave there will be fresh rhema, healing, deliverance, purging, cleansing, and restoration. Those who have gotten stale, living a life of unrighteousness, think they got it all together. This wave is going to tear down the wall of denominational barriers. A wave of disturbance (it's going to upset, trouble, and interrupt) shake people who really thought they were being used by God. Remember the counterfeiter, the pretender, and the imitator. June 11, at 10:30 p.m., again the Lord spoke and said this wave will be a new awareness of spiritual gifts, not just ordinary gifts.

June 12, at approximately 5:50 p.m., the Lord spoke again. In this wave, it's going to be miraculous healing and deliverance, extraordinary, and unusual manifestation of divine supernatural power of the almighty God. It's going to be some rough waves within the wave. The rough, tough, strong waves, again no one can stop this wave (this movement of God). It's going to tear down; it's going to build up. It's going to be awesome. In this wave, it's going to be judgment, what is real and what is false.

Reaching the Community with the Love of God

In January 1999, Morning Revival Ministries launched its first quarterly mini-magazine "For God's Glory!" To promote community health and spiritual awareness, many programs were initiated to foster families, marriages, youth, education, and health workshops. The quarterly magazine facilitated more than two hundred readers. Community events included prayer rallies, tribute to mothers events, prayer and family breakfasts, and fellowship. These activities were the heart of the ministry's plan to help those who truly want to rebuild their lives spiritually, physically, and mentally.

CHAPTER 14

Rose Fiftieth Birthday Gala
March 1999

But he that is married careth for the things that
are of the world, how he may please *his* wife.

—1 Corinthians 7:33 (KJV)

The beginning of 1999 got off to an awesome start. I have
been observing my loving husband who have been saving
money for that special day—my fiftieth birthday celebration. I watched how he and the children made plans, in
search of ways to surprise me—which was not very easy!
However, the biggest surprise was, while I was getting
dressed, low and behold, as I walked out of my room, I saw
a chauffeur sitting in my living room—I was blown away—
not knowing what was next. As my husband and I exited
the door, sitting in our driveway was a cream Rolls-Royce!
The chauffeur held the car door opened for us and then got
into the driver's seat and off went cruising down "lover's
lane," sitting in the back close together, with all eyes on us.

Bystanders and people in passing traffic just stared at us, maybe assuming we were some big celebrities!!!! Well, their assumptions were right; we were celebrities of the almighty God. Amen. I really felt very special. We arrived at the hall. What a surprise, there were so many family and friends, food, and gifts, what a celebration. What a special time, my husband and children showed their appreciation for me— one that I will remember for a lifetime. As the old saying goes, "When God made my husband, he threw away the mold," there will never be another Samuel John Strong Jr.

> Husbands, love your wives as Christ loved the church and gave his life for it. He did this to make the church holy by cleansing it, washing it using water along with spoken words. Then he could present it to himself as a glorious church, without any kind of stain or wrinkle—holy and without faults. So, husbands must love their wives as they love their own bodies. A man who loves his wife loves himself. No one ever hated his own body. Instead, he feeds and takes care of it, as Christ takes care of the church. We are parts of his body. That's why a man will leave his father and mother and be united with his wife, and the two will be one. This is a great mystery. (I'm talking about Christ's relationship to the church.) But every husband must love his wife as he loves himself, and wives

should respect their husbands. (Ephesians 5:25–33, GW)

As the above scripture states, I can honestly say my husband (Samuel John Strong, Jr) exemplified the scriptures in our marriage, family, ministry, and his daily walk with the Lord. He was a godly husband, not just reading the scriptures but applying them in his daily life. He did not just say he loved me, he demonstrated his love in action, as were manifested in the scripture.

Mommy Dearest

To the mom I love whom no one can replace. In which my heart will always have space. For all the times you showed me you cared. If no one else I knew, you'd be there. Words can't express what I feel inside. And my love for thee, I will never hide. When you see me now, you can rest assured. For Life's struggle has made me mature. If I had one wish, do you know what it will be? That my dearest Mom live out all her dreams. I Love You Mom. Your hard work paid off.

Samuel John Strong, III

Bundle of Joy

In June 18, 1999, my husband and I were blessed with our first granddaughter. This was indeed a time of rejoicing for our family as we waited to see this gorgeous baby girl enter the world. Our hearts were filled with much joy as we helped caring for her and watched her developed from stage to stage. In our home, she was always the center of attention. We didn't mind, and we cherished the moments.

Working Together, United We Stand

While attending college, my husband and I continued doing outreach ministry. Our younger generation was of major concern; we endeavored to see our youth use their talents constructively, instead of in a destructive manner. We recognized the potential and visions our children had and where they needed assistance in fulfilling them. Also, the vision was to help better our neighborhoods, communities, and cities by bringing restoration to marriages and families and deliverance and hope to those who are abused and bound by the powers of evil. Although I was still attending college, my husband and I refused to allow this to stop us from serving others. We continued to reach the total man with compassion, love, deliverance, and hope for the glory of God.

Empowerment 2000–2003

Between 2000 and 2003, after graduating from Trinity International University, I continued my education in marriage and family therapy at St. Thomas University. Although it was a Catholic university, it was an awesome time of learning, meeting new people, and nice professors, most of whom were of great encouragement to me.

My internship which was centered around families and child enrichment was a tremendous experience. I had the opportunity to put what I had learned into action. However, after graduating with my master's degree in 2003, I was offered a job with the same agency. It was very enjoyable working as an in-home crisis intervention therapist. I worked one-on-one with countless families (some of whom have had similar encounters) and seen numerous neglects and physical, sexual, mental/verbal, and drug abuse, as well as abandonment of children and families. I have witnessed domestic violence, violence on individuals, gun violence, anger, and disciplinary issues in the lives of children and families. As a result, I had firsthand experience when it came to parenting and discipline. When a child is disciplined by the use of objects or punching to the body or head, that is no longer considered discipline; rather, this is domestic violence on the child, especially when the child is very young and cannot fight back. Hence, this kind of abuse on a child often results in irreparable physical, emotional, and mental damages throughout that child's life.

No one knows what the future holds. However, as believers in Christ, we know God almighty holds our future, and he knows what each of us will encounter throughout life.

*****

January 6, 2002. Solid Rock Redemptive Ministries Church, Inc. became an established congregation. Solid Rock Redemptive Ministries is an outreach organization geared toward bringing change to its audience, which includes: individuals, marriages, families and youths.

In 2003, my husband and I were ordained as pastor and elder of Solid Rock Redemptive Ministries Church.

Love Was In the Air

January 2004 was the beginning of an exciting year. I started planning ahead for the special day, our thirty-second marriage anniversary, not knowing that in eight months my husband would no longer be here with me. Throughout my planning, here and there, it seemed as if I was planning for a wedding. It was a feeling of great excitement looking forward to something very, very special. In the past years, if our anniversary fell on a weekday, we would celebrate on the weekend. However, this anniversary was so special. I wanted to celebrate it on the actual day which was on a Tuesday, March 11.

During my time of planning, I checked with his principal, and I explained to her what I would like to do for our anniversary on his job. She agreed with my plans and explained to me that it was okay. Also, I checked with my supervisor and expressed to her that it was out anniversary and I would like to use the chapel for our anniversary celebration. She gave me the okay to set up the table in the chapel. My husband was not aware of my plans because I really wanted to surprise him and to do something very special for both of us on that day. I ordered two cakes from Publix and had them custom made to look like a real wedding cake. In order to have coworkers celebrate with us, I took one cake to my husband's job and the other to my job.

On that special day, March 11, 2004, I started in the morning by presenting him with a special-made anniversary card for him to throw him off. We wished each other happy anniversary and off to work we went. Excited about surprising him, I picked up the cakes from Publix, took one to my job, and set it up—it looked just like a wedding reception cake table.

Coworkers would come by, wished us happy anniversary, signed our card, and get a slice of cake and some Hershey Kisses.

The time came for me to leave and go to his job, still excited and looking forward to seeing this man whom I love so much (my husband). I wanted to really surprise him on this special day. I arrived at his job and one of the students (office aid) assisted me in bringing in the cake, chips, drinks, etc., to his room during his planning period. When we knocked on the door, to his surprise, he saw my face, the cake, etc. His coworkers came by, wished us happy anniversary, chatted a while, and took a piece a cake and off they went.

Now, school was over, we went home, relaxed for a while, and celebrated our wedding anniversary, again, at home. Our children came over, wished us happy anniversary, and blessed us with a gift certificate to go to dinner in an exclusive, high-class restaurant for that evening. It was now time for us to prepare and go out to our last dinner celebration for the day. Now we are both excited, holding hands on our way to this very special dinner date.

Upon arrival at the restaurant, we were greeted with smiles and congratulations. We both felt very honored. We had our own personal attendant who escorted and served us at our special table. It was a spectacular night—very romantic! All this time, I was bubbling over with such joy and anticipation, eager to surprise my husband with his special anniversary gift. I was not concerned about what he was giving me, because he always gave me money or expensive perfume. I was more concerned about making him so happy on this special day. Now, it was time to present him with his gift. He did not see me taking the gift inside—knowing me, I can be very creative! I had carried his gift under my arm, in my jacket. When I finally gave him his gift, he was so amazed. I could see the expression of happiness and love displayed upon his face—it was an unexplainable moment!!! It was an awesome night. We both really enjoyed ourselves. Weeks and months later, we talked about our anniversary, the excitement, our love for each other, the surprises, and more. This anniversary was the best we had since we were married. Others were good but this was the best one. We fell in love more with each other, but it was something special about this anniversary. We were two happy people deeply in love.

Joy in the Mist of the Storm

*****

He was diagnosed with congestive heart failure (CHF) several years before. Nevertheless, he did not allow that to be a drawback in his life. Around the month of July, he went to a funeral in another town, upon returning home, he became ill and was hospitalized for CHF. After spending some time in the hospital, he was released and sent home. Days later, he returned back to work. He appeared to be doing well and excited about getting back into the classroom.

However, again, in August, he faced another challenge with CHF and was hospitalized for several more days. In spite of that, he was determined not to allow the challengers to alter his life. So passionate to serve, he returned to the classroom. It was such joy for him to see the students learn. However, I believe, it was his faith and love for God, me, family, and others that motivated him not to give up.

Genesis Shockwave September 2004–2007

September started off great, although there were a few challenges. He was again admitted to the hospital for congestive heart failure. However, after several days, he was released and went back to work.

Saturday, September 18, in the wee hours of the morning, I was awakened by a very disturbing dream/vision. I knew in the vision that someone would be departing from this earthly life. I got up, called one of my prayer partners, and shared the vision with her. We began warfare praying, speaking the Word of God, rebuking the spirit of death, and claiming life for my husband and other family members, not knowing who it was. Ironically, I dealt with the vision throughout the day. I even called the presiding bishop. Later that evening, the bishop came over to pray for us. My sister-in-law also came over. The bishop sat with my husband for quite some time; they shared spiritual information, and he prayed with my husband. My husband looked happy that he and the bishop shared that time together.

Sunday, September 19, 2004

This day was a special day for us; we were feeling good spiritually and emotionally and excited about the worship service hours ahead. We were still so much in love with each other. During worship service, I could see my husband standing with his hand raised, worshipping God and listening to the Word of God. We served communion to the congregation and then served each other, which was awesome. I believe that he knew he was getting ready to leave me, based on the expressions on his face as well as some of the things he said. One thing he said that really stuck with me was, "I'm so glad I went to church today."

After we got home from service, we rested for a little while and then went out for dinner. On our way to the restaurant, I kept thinking about the conversation we had on our way from church. Again, reflecting back, I believe my husband had a premonition about leaving me. After dinner, we went home and we sat on one corner of our section sofa, very close together, as we talked about our children and family. He mentioned how proud he was of our two children, his son and his daughter. He was especially grateful that God had allowed him to live to see them grow up and be independent and productive children. Thinking back, I believe he was trying to tell me something. Looking back, I guess I would say it was a conversation and a good-bye. Overall, it was a great day indeed!

My Rose, I Will Be Leaving You Today!

Monday, September 20, 2004, my husband and I woke up with such joy; we both had a light breakfast. Since he had been in the hospital several weeks before and the doctor had placed him on a no-salt and limited liquids diet, he was not too happy about the cream of wheat, because he could not have salt. On the other hand, we sat around talking about today's agenda. I agreed to take the car to have the battery replaced. The car would not start, so I called my brother Joe who came to our rescue. Off to the mall I went to get a new battery. When I returned home several hours later, my husband appeared to be fine. He did not complain about any pain or any shortness of breath; however, he appeared just a little weak, due to the change in his diet.

He was sitting comfortably in our custom-made sectional recliner. While waiting to do my home visits with clients, I recalled our last conversation. However, he needed something from the pharmacy, so I agreed to go and pick it up for him. It was approximately 2:45–2:55 p.m. when I left my husband sitting in his recliner, looking over some paperwork. Reflecting back, he could have been making sure that legally everything was in order. My last words to him were "Okay, sweetheart, I'll see you shortly" or "I'll be right back."

With a smile on his face, he looked up and said, "Okay!" So off to the store I went—less than five minutes from where we lived.

To my amazement, I returned home about 3:15 p.m., and he was not sitting in the recliner where I had left him. Hurriedly, I started walking down the hallway, I called "Sam, I'm back." I repeated, "Sam, I'm back." Still, no response. I walked into our bedroom repeating, "I'm back." He did not respond. I flipped the light on, and there was my husband lying in bed. I called him again, he did not respond. I rushed onto the bed and began shaking and pushing him, no response. Frantically, I began screaming, crying, and calling him—telling him to wake up—but no response. Approximately at 3:15 p.m., my life changed without anyone's permission. I lost it! I began crying, asking God, "Is this what you were showing me on Saturday?" I was crying hysterically. I panicked. I dialed 911 from my cell phone. Crying and trying to do what I was directed to do as the dispatcher gave me instructions, suddenly, we got disconnected. Quickly, I redialed. They gave me instructions, but he would not wake up.

Minutes later the rescue arrived. They tried to resuscitate him. They put him on the stretcher and took him to the hospital. As I arrived at the hospital, other family members joined me, waiting and hoping for the good news. A little while later, the doctor entered the waiting area and announced to us that he was deceased. I cannot explain the pain, the grief, the crying, and the tears in the room when we got the news. At that moment, I cannot express what I felt—a pain I had never experienced before, in my entire life. I started thinking, *My husband, the shoulder I would lean on, the man of God who I loved so dearly, the father of our children, my friend, my partner in ministry, the man who took care of me, and was there for me, now he is gone?* I felt weak. I had no strength—now what do I do? Who do I lean on? Not only was I in shock. I was in denial. This was just too unreal but, on the other hand, it was reality—he really is gone, the man I loved, my friend, the one that I shared so many precious moments with, my head covering, etc.

The Secret of Life
To My Loving Husband

I'm glad we took time to think together; it strengthened our relationship.

I'm glad we took time to pray and worship the Lord together in love.

I'm glad we took time to be friendly to each other; it was the road to the happiness we shared.

I'm glad we took time to work; it was the price of success.

I'm glad we took time to pray; it was the greatest power of the earth.

I'm glad we took time to forgive, for it strengthened our marriage.

I'm glad we took time to spend time together, for we experienced a true love.

I'm glad we took time to love and be loved, for it was the way of God.

Though I am glad, I will miss the door opening for your arrival at 4:15 p.m.

Though I am glad, I will miss watching the 10:00 o'clock news with you.

Thought I am glad, I will miss you letting out your recliner while I'm letting out mine.

Though I am glad, I will miss us shopping and doing all the things we enjoyed together.

Though I am glad, I will miss the path you made from your side of the bed to mine; it is fading.

Though I am glad, I will miss your embrace, your touch and your kiss…

Love, Your Rose!

I am now in a place of desolation, a place of gloominess. I felt so troubled in my spirits, a mournfulness of heartache and distress. The grief seemed unbearable, the pain, the agony, the anguish, and the suffering, it still seemed unreal. I believe I would have given anything to change what happened on this day. However, there was nothing I could do to flip the situation. In the midst of it all, I depended on God—and only God at this moment gave me the strength to endure. As families, neighbors, brothers, and sisters in the Lord came to give their condolences, expressions on their faces revealed the deep pain and sorrow they felt. I believe if they could have taken some of the pain and the grief that they saw me going through, they would have. This is when I really understood what God's Word meant when it says, "Until death do you part." At this moment, it seemed that a part of me was gone.

Planning for the home-going service was the most difficult time in my life. In the meantime, I had to do what was needed. The family came together overwhelming to help with the obituary and the program.

Twelve days later, we gathered together to go to the church for the service, again this was so difficult for me— so much pain—but thank God he enabled me to make it through each day. After the service, the visitations started to cease, not many more phone calls, and home visits also started to fade. Realizing people had their own daily agendas and responsibilities, I realized now that I must face reality and start adjusting to this new chapter in my life. However, I know it would not be easy and will take years to get back my daily routines. With God, the prayers of the saints, and support from ministry and families, I knew that I could make it through this difficult time of my life. I witnessed God turned many difficult situations triumphantly. Therefore, my trust, my faith, a ndmy confidence were in him. At times, when I could not even pray, I would just say his name, "Jesus."

> And he spoke a parable unto them *to this end,* that men ought *always* to pray, and not to faint. (Luke 18:1, KJV)

> Pray without ceasing. (1 Thessalonians 5:17, KJV)

This is why we, as believers, should pray not just when we need something special from God or just a religious duty. There will come a time in life where you can only whisper the name of Jesus. This is why we are commissioned to *pray without ceasing.* It is wise to store up prayer in advance. I am confident that the prayers of intercessions were advanced prayers for such times as this in my life. God promised he will never leave us nor forsake us. God assured us that he is always with us. Amen.

Widowhood

> For this cause shall a man leave his father
> and mother, and cleave to his wife;
> And they twain shall be one flesh: so then
> they are no more twain, but one flesh.

What therefore God hath joined together,
let not man put asunder.

—Mark 10:7-9 (KJV)

Weeks later, most of my family members returned to their respective cities and states. Now I am home alone for real. There were many challenges I faced while being home alone. Starting a new lifestyle—"a widow's lifestyle"—was not easy, knowing that my husband was in heaven. In the meantime, I must go on—and this is what he would have wanted me to do. I must say, in the midst of my distress, what I was going through, I never lost my faith. I trusted in God. I knew that God was there with me all the time. He promised he would never leave me nor forsake me.

For months I was grief-stricken. At times I felt I could not make it through another day. I cried incessantly. For days I would not eat—sometimes I even forget to eat. Mentally, many times I was not in the frame of mind to handle personal matters. As I recalled, one night the grief was so heavy. As I sat at my dining room table, I felt as if I was getting ready to leave this world. Suddenly, I remembered the previous words God had spoken into my spirit that I would not die but live to declare the works of the Lord. I knew I had too much to live for and did not need to be home alone. As a result, I called my brother, and he picked me up at nights after he gets off work and takes me to his home. Then I would spend the night with him and his family and return home in the mornings.

Being there with my brother and his family was a great blessing; it helped to ease my grief. Prayer and sharing also helped me immensely in the healing process. When my brother would bring me back home the next morning, I would try to sort out legal and personal matters each day. With the help of the Holy Spirit, I believe I did a pretty good job! I give all the glory to God for helping me during those hard times.

After some time away, I went back to work. Again, I knew that I was not going to be this way always. However, while I hope for things to get much better, I still found myself in a pool of grief. On the other hand, I found some comfort helping others through their times of hardship. Many days I sat at my desk and cried. The tears would just roll from my eyes over my mouth as I wrote my progress notes. Seemingly, the grief was unbearable, but I kept fighting the good fight of faith and trusting in God to help me, because he was the only one that could do so.

It is amazing how all things work together for good. Although my grief was still devastating, when I realized that several of my clients were on their death bed, I quickly put aside my grief and my situation and moved toward helping others through a difficult time of their life. God knew what I was going through. Helping others seemed to have strengthened me. On my way to do home visits, at times, I didn't know where I was going. At times, I would drive for miles and miles, crying and asking God to help me. Eventually, the Holy Spirit would lead me to my destination. Despite all of my grief, I kept on fighting the good fight of faith.

Working a full-time job and caring for the ministry was not easy. Months later, I took a leave of absence, hoping that this would ease the pain. Looking for comfort and support from the ministry that we were both connected to later served as a great disappointment. The minister had openly vowed to their congregation and our congregation that our ministry would be leasing their building once they move into their new building. We spent countless hours cleaning the building—not counting the money we spent—getting it ready for us to move in. Our congregation was all looking forward to moving in.

Suddenly, as time went by, the disappointments, letdowns, and broken promises were another blow in the midst of a grieving congregation and myself as the leader. How do I share this "breaking news"? This, too, was very painful, adding more to the grief. I had to really trust in the Word of God. In the midst of a painful situation, I refused to be bitter and unforgiving. I must say it was extremely difficult for our congregation, knowing they would do such injustice to those that loved and served God faithfully. However, as we continue to trust God, he enabled us to find another place to worship. Without a doubt, we had no choice but to depend on God!

On the other hand, I recall, it was an awesome day and study time. I was led by the Spirit of God to research the following scriptures on "widows." After the study, I felt very special and closer to the heart of God. It was comforting to know that God was really taking good care of me in "widowhood." Also, I am thanking God for the faithful members and partners he has provided for the ministry.

They all were there for me and stood with me in fighting the good fight of faith. God did great things through Solid Rock Redemptive Ministries. Many lives were saved and delivered.

Widows and Orphans
Hold a Special place in God's Heart

Scriptures of Encouragement:

> The Lord tears down the house of an arrogant person, but he protects the property of widows. (Proverbs 15:25, GW)

The Word of God demands that widows must be treated with kindness (Exodus 22:22; Deuteronomy 14:29). Was I treated with kindness by those who claimed to be my covering? No—I was not! The reason I am sharing this is to encourage you to be true to God and yourself as well as with your brothers and sisters in the Lord when you encounter injustice from anyone. While I am not saying for you to be a doormat, I encourage you to stand firm in faith and watch God work for you!

> If you do and they cry out to me, (God) you can be sure that I will hear their cry. (Exodus 22:23, GW)

> The Lord protects foreigners. The Lord gives relief to orphans and widows. But he

keeps wicked people from reaching their goal. (Psalms 146:9, GW)

A widow who has no family has placed her confidence in God by praying and asking for his help night and day. (1 Timothy 5:5, GW)

He makes sure orphans and widows receive justice. He loves foreigners and gives them food and clothes. (Deuteronomy 10:18, GW)

The God who is in his holy dwelling place is the father of the fatherless and the defender of widows. (Psalms 68:5, GW)

The Lord protects foreigners. The Lord gives relief to orphans and widows. But he keeps wicked people from reaching their goal. (Psalms 146:9, GW)

Ye shall not afflict any widow, or fatherless child. (Exodus 22:22, KJV)

Elevator Jammed, 2008

Just the time I was beginning to really get back to what I would call a normal life, another storm erupted. Working a little late one evening, I took the elevator from the car garage back to my office. I stepped in and pushed the elevator button—nothing happened! After pressing the button several times, the elevator door still would not open. Evidently, I panicked; after pressing the emergency button, kicking, and trying to force the door open, I began passing out but was able to call 911 rescue. They came and plowed the door open. I was taken to the hospital, checked out, and later released. Consequently, I spent several weeks in therapy and doctors' visits but continued working. However, I realized it was a little too much of a strain on my life. Overall, I knew I had to make a decision.

In 2009, I resigned from my job. Some would say, "By now she should be over the loss." I realized that I was still in a state of grief. I did not want to be home alone, so I purchased a little *shih tzu dog Tea`Ko*. Therapeutically, this helped me a lot. I was able to start focusing on ministry and my personal life.

Again, in 2010, I had another storm. On my way to an appointment, I was involved in a "total loss" car accident. Praise be unto God, I emerged with only a sprained ankle—not one scratch or broken bone. Also, the driver of the other car was not injured. Thank God for his protection and the angels that he had encamped around me while I was driving.

CHAPTER 15

The Birthing of Urban and Community Outreach Squad (UCOS)

UCOS is a division of Solid Rock Redemptive Ministries, birth in 2011. UCOS is an organized team of people from the community, ages five years and older, that realized "enough is enough." Its mission is to assist in helping to take back our cities, communities, schools, and neighborhoods by providing safe alternatives for reducing the necessity of our youth to resort to gang memberships, drugs, and violence in their quest for love.

It's a team of people not just talking the talk about what is happening in our communities and cities but put forth effort to bring change. This is a team of people with compassion for individuals, families, youth, and children regardless of age, race, or gender.

It's a dedicated team committed to spreading agape love—the love of Jesus—in talking the talk and walking the walk in our neighborhoods, schools, communities, and cities.

UCOS aims to prevent violence before it spreads in the home at an early age.

UCOS will educate individuals, families, children, and youth on the importance of being a productive citizen. It's a team of prayer and much more. I now understand what was prophesied to me on August 23, 1992, concerning different areas of the ministry.

More Blessed to Give

In 2011 I have always had a heart to give and serve. After becoming a believer in Christ Jesus, my desire became much stronger. I honestly can say I do not recall ever not giving tithes or offerings in any worship service. However, the Word of God is true when it states in Luke 6:38 (GW), "Give and you will receive." God promised a large quantity, pressed down, shaken, and running over, will be given back. In plain truth, the standards you use for others will be applied to you.

Not boasting, I just like to give a financial testimony on how God blessed me. My next-door neighbors moved away to another state. The owners of the home contacted me and asked me if I wanted to buy the house. After checking with my son, telling him that they were asking us if we wanted to buy the house, he thought it was a good deal. So I bought the house for $40,000. This particular house was a 3/2, very nice house, in a great neighborhood, and in good condition. After everything was finalized, I rented out the house for approximately three years. Later the house was sold for four times plus more than I bought it for. Now that is increase!. Evidently, God kept his promise—"pressed down, shaken, and running over!" He truly multiplied in this and many other cases. It was a tremendous blessing; it pays to be a giver in the kingdom of God.

> Each of you should give whatever you have decided. You shouldn't be sorry that you gave or feel forced to give, since God loves a cheerful giver. Besides, God will give you his constantly overflowing kindness. Then, when you always have everything you need, you can do more and more good things. Scripture says, "The person with God's approval gives freely to the poor. The things he does with God's approval continue forever." (2 Corinthians 9:7-9, GW) Corinthians 9:7,GW)

It is not always the amount that we give—as long as we give cheerfully. This is only a testimony to share how God rewarded me. I believe it is because of my love, honesty, and faithfulness to him and love and care for others.

Ministry Transition

Solid Rock Redemptive Ministries (SRRMC) consisted of approximately 85 percent family and 15 percent nonfamily members. It was such a joy seeing family members coming to Christ and continuing to serve him. But on the other hand, as in any family, there will be some family pain. I could say it was not easy ministering to mostly family members.

In 2012 and 2013, however, the ministry started going through financial difficulties. Once we started facing these challenges, I knew we (the leaders) had to make some firm decisions on how to keep the rent and monthly bills paid. In the meantime, we persevered, believing God to provide a way for SRRMC, to continue attending worship services and serving the community at large. Our financial crisis came as a result of a decrease in church membership and finances. After much prayer and fasting, sharing with other ministers in the gospel, and explaining to them some of the things SRRMC was encountering, we all came to a mutual understanding, as they, too, had gone through similar situations. This was a great encouragement to me and the SRRMC congregation.

January 2014 arrived with a little different twist than the past years. On this particular day, January 2, I received a rhema word from God. As I meditated and worshipped, I realized that the grief, sadness, disappointments, and other concerns I was dealing with was starting to diminish. The more I paid attention to God's direction concerning the transitioning of the ministry, the more the Spirit of God began to speak to me.

On January 18, 2014, approximately 2:35 p.m., as I was getting dressed to run a couple of errands, the Spirit of God began to speak to my spirit. God said, "I know the past nine years were very difficult. I saw everything you went through, the tears, the love for others, the sacrifices, the self-neglect, your faithfulness, your prayers, and your requests." This brought much comfort and confirmation to me, just knowing that God was always with me through it all in this ministry transition.

January 26, 2014, was our final service at that location. In the meantime, Solid Rock Redemptive Ministries, and those who wished, fellowshipped with a local ministry until we started services in a house we were waiting to rent. We rendered faithful worship services and other community events at the house.

Don't Give Up

In late 2015, SRRMC had to move from the house we were using for ministry services, as the property was up for sale. During the time of ministry transitioning, I did not know what I would encounter—only God knew!!! I was led to serve at another church where I fellowshipped in the p.m. services. As the Spirit of God continued directing me to this ministry, I started attending both a.m. and p.m. services. Not knowing what was in store for me, I encountered rejection from some of the people. This was nothing new to me. Of course, I did not welcome neither the spiritual nor emotional pains that were imposed upon me.

Despite the circumstances, trusting God—and God only—was my ultimate goal. Hence, I was not going to allow the mistreatment of a few people to turn me away from God or to stop serving God in this ministry, for that matter. Although things got a little better with time, I remained steadfast in fighting the good fight of faith by trusting and obeying God's Word and his promises.

Even so, I had no idea or ever thought of what God had in store for me during the transitioning of the ministry. I was serious about getting married again. I took my request to God in prayer and explained to him what I desired in this man of God. After letting my request known, I continued on my journey doing some outreach ministry with Solid Rock Redemptive Ministries and serving, at times, in the ministry where I worshipped.

CHAPTER 16

Starting a New Chapter

In December 3, 2016, God answered my prayers—I met my current husband at a prayer breakfast, and on July 28, 2017, we got married. I felt compelled to bring closure to the incident that happened to me as a little girl in 1965. Reflecting back through the years, I often wondered of the whereabouts of the young lady who witnessed the two guys forcing me into their car. Whenever I spoke to someone who knew her, they would say, "She lives in another city." Well, I knew I was not going to look for her because I'm pretty sure it would have raised some questions as to why I wanted to visit her. Psalms 37:4 (GW) says, "Be happy with the *Lord*, and he will give you the desires of your heart."

It's Never Too Late

August 2017, one of my nieces who lived in the same town where the incident occurred in 1965. She accepted the Lord in 1995 had passed away. My new husband and I went to the home-going service. During family visitation, I recognized the young lady who was also visiting at the home. Refreshing my memory, I asked her where she lived originally. She replied, "I had moved away, but I moved back to this town." Immediately, I realized that where she lived was not far from the house where the abduction took place in 1965. I tell you, the memories, the house looked the same, except for larger trees with the roots spreading all over the yard.

As my husband and I were on our way back home to Florida, in my heart I knew that I had to go back and speak with this young lady at a more opportune time. In the meantime, I coupled with one of my prayer partners, fasting and praying about having a future visit with this young lady and hoping that she would be truthful about the situation.

After much prayer and fasting, God made a way for my husband and me to return to that city. While we were there, I asked God to make a way for me to meet with this young lady. God is so awesome! As we visited with a family member in the vicinity, the same young lady came over. I knew that this was the perfect opportunity for me to confront her and shared with her what had been on my heart for fifty-two years. Moving forward, as we sat around in the house and talked, the young lady got up and excused herself. She exclaimed, "I need to go on the porch and smoke a cigarette." Right then and there, I knew that this was my moment. So I got up and immediately went out on the porch where she was sitting. Although it was cold outside, I was willing to sit there and share with her. I began to explain the situation to her. At first she tried to deny it, saying she did not remember. I explained to her verbatim what happened that fateful night in 1965. When she realized that she could no longer continue to deny the facts, she stated, "I do remember!!!" Immediately, her demeanor changed. I could see the regret on her face, wishing she had done something at that time to prevent a lifetime of sorrow.

> Therefore I say unto you, "What things soever ye desire, when ye pray, believe that ye receive *them*, and ye shall have *them*. And when ye stand praying, forgive, if ye have ought against any: that your Father also which is in heaven may forgive you your trespasses. But if ye do not forgive, neither will your Father which is in heaven forgive your trespasses." (Mark 11:24–26, KJV)

Although, I had forgiven her, thank God after more than fifty-two years, I was able to share face-to-face the baggage I had carried for so long.

Closing

As I closed this chapter of my life, I pray that you will be encouraged not to give up. As a child of God, we will have tests, trials, and tribulations. According to 2 Corinthians 4:8–9 (KJV); We are troubled on every side, yet not distressed; we are perplexed, but not in despair; Persecuted, but not forsaken; cast down, but not destroyed; Despite the many roadblocks I encountered, I refused to let that stop me from trusting God. Therefore, I encourage you to do the same. Do not allow the circumstances of life to hinder you from reaching your God-given life purpose. Please remember, God promised he will never leave us nor forsake us—a promise he does keep!!!

According to God's Word in Isaiah 43:1–5:

> The Lord created Jacob and formed Israel. Now, this is what the Lord says, "Do not be afraid, because I have reclaimed you. I have called you by name; you are mine. When you go through the sea, I am with you. When you go through the rivers, they will not sweep you away. When you walk through fire, you will not be burned, and the flames will not harm you. I am the Lord your God, the Holy One of Israel, your Savior. I am the Lord your God, the Holy One of Israel, your Savior. Egypt is the ransom I exchanged for you. Sudan and Seba are the price I paid for you.
>
> Since you are precious to me, you are honored and I love you. I will exchange others for you. Nations will be the price I pay for your life.
>
> Do not be afraid, because I am with you. I will bring your descendants from the east and gather you from the west."

Now visually impaired, I refuse to allow a disability to hinder my capability. Rather, I feel even more challenged and highly motivated to encourage others, expectantly others with any disability will be inspired to pursue their dreams in life.

CHAPTER 17

Scriptures of Encouragement

Righteous people cry out. The Lord hears and rescues them from all their troubles. The Lord is near to those whose hearts are humble. He saves those whose spirits are crushed. The righteous person has many troubles, but the Lord rescues him from all of them. (Psalms 34:17–19, GW)

Blessed are those who are persecuted for doing what God approves of. The king-dom of heaven belongs to them. Blessed are you when people insult you, persecute you, lie, and say all kinds of evil things about you because of me. Rejoice and be glad because you have a great reward in heaven! The prophets who lived before you were persecuted in these ways. (Matthew 5:10–12, GW)

I've told you this so that my peace will be with you. In the world you'll have trouble. But cheer up! I have overcome the world. (John 16:33, GW)

The one who loves us gives us an overwhelming victory in all these difficulties. I am convinced that nothing can ever separate us from God's love which Christ Jesus our Lord shows us. We can't be separated by death or life, by angels or rulers, by anything in the present or anything in the future, by forces or powers in the world above or in the world below, or by anything else in creation. (Romans 8:37–39, GW)

But he told me, "My kindness is all you need. My power is strongest when you are weak." So I will brag even more about my weaknesses in order that Christ's power will live in me. (2 Corinthians 12:9 GW)

Jesus was made a little lower than the angels, but we see him crowned with glory and honor because he suffered death. Through God's kindness he died on behalf of everyone. (Hebrews 2:9, GW)

He chose to suffer with God's people rather than to enjoy the pleasures of sin for a little while. (Hebrews 11:25, GW)

Brothers and sisters, follow the example of the prophets who spoke in the name of the Lord. They were patient when they suffered unjustly. We consider those who endure to be blessed. You have heard about Job's endurance. You saw that the Lord ended Job's suffering because the Lord is compassionate and merciful. (5:10–11, GW)

God is pleased if a person is aware of him while enduring the pains of unjust suffering.

What credit do you deserve if you endure a beating for doing something wrong? But if you endure suffering for doing something good, God is pleased with you.

God called you to endure suffering because Christ suffered for you. He left you an example so that you could follow in his footsteps. (1 Peter 2:19–21, GW)

Who will harm you if you are devoted to doing what is good? But even if you suffer for doing what God approves, you are blessed. Don't be afraid of those who want to harm you. Don't get upset. But dedicate your lives to Christ as Lord. Always be ready to defend your confidence in God when anyone asks you to explain it. However, make your defense with gentleness and respect. Keep your conscience clear. Then those who treat the good Christian life you live with contempt will feel ashamed that they have ridiculed you. After all, if it is God's will, it's better to suffer for doing good than for doing wrong. (1 Peter 3:13–17, GW)

Dear friends, don't be surprised by the fiery troubles that are coming in order to test you. Don't feel as though something strange is happening to you, but be happy as you share Christ's sufferings. Then you will also be full of joy when he appears again in his glory. If you are insulted because of the name of Christ, you are blessed because the Spirit of glory—the Spirit of God—is resting on you. If you suffer, you shouldn't suffer for being a murderer, thief, criminal, or troublemaker. If you suffer for being a Christian, don't feel ashamed, but praise God for being called that name. (1 Peter 4:12–16, GW)

Faith Confessions

1. I have what I think, believe, speak, and act according to God's Word.
2. I live in God and his Word lives in me.
3. I am confident that God listens to me when I pray.
4. I speak out what the Word of God says.
5. I walk in love and forgiveness.
6. I walk in health and healing.
7. I walk in the Spirit and not in the flesh.
8. I walk in blessings, not in curses.
9. I am strong in the Lord and in the power of his might.
10. I am a cheerful giver of my finances.
11. I walk and live by faith and not by sight.
12. I am confident that no weapon formed against me shall prosper.
13. I am an heir of God and joint heir with Christ.
14. I am a winner, not a loser in the name of Jesus. Amen.

By: RS 2016

God is With You!

Israel, the LORD who created you says,
"Do not be afraid—I will save you. I have
Called you by name—you are mine.
When you pass through deep waters, I
will be with you; your troubles will not
overwhelm you. When you pass through
fire, you will not be burned; the hard trials
that come will not hurt you. For I am the
LORD your God, the holy God of Israel, who
saves you. . . .
Isaiah 43:1-3 (GNT)

"I have told you these things, so that in me you may
have peace. In this world you will have trouble.
But take heart! I have overcome the world.
John 16:33 (NIV)

CONCLUSION

Thank you for reading this part of my autobiography. I pray you were encouraged and will share my story with someone that may be going through a very difficult time in their life.

May God continue to grant you the desires of your heart, according to his Word.

Combination

Designed by: Rhodessia

My Baby Picture

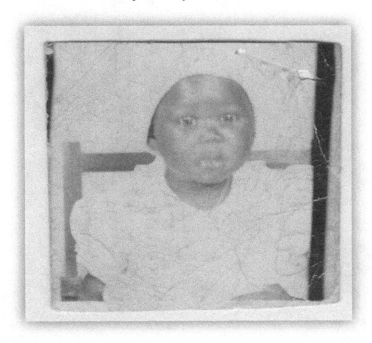

My Teenage Years

He Served His Country Well

Sandie and Samuel III

Sandie and Samuel III

Samuel Jr, Rose, Sandie and Samuel III

My Twenties

Special Occasions

Staff/Trips

Education

ST. THOMAS UNIVERSITY
Commencement Ceremony
May 8, 2004

Evening of Romance

Dorcas Fashions Designs by: Rhodessia

Prayer Warriors

June 1984 and December 11, 1994 Ordinations

Teaching on The Meaning of Baptism
Acts 2:38; Romans 6:4
1 Peter 3:21

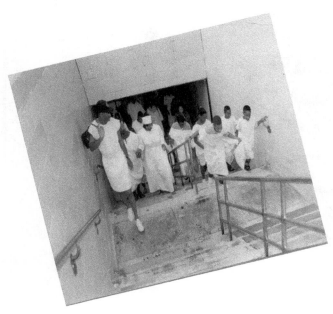

O' What a Glorious Day!

The Power of God Is Greater Than Any Other Force

Victorious Baptism

Radio Broadcasting

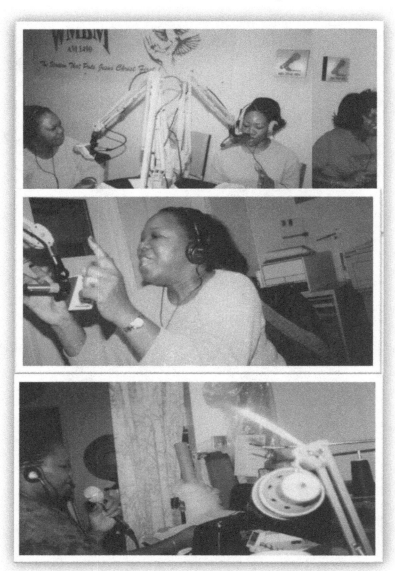

Broadcasting From My Sewing, Prayer And Workroom

Community Outreach

Morning Revival Ministries

Solid Rock Redemptive Ministries

We Must Bare Our Cross

SRRMC Baptism Pics

Then Jesus came to them and said, "All authority in heaven and on earth has been given to me. 19 Therefore go and make disciples of all nations, baptizing them in the name of the Father and of the Son and of the Holy Spirit, 20 and teaching them to obey everything I have commanded you. And surely, I am with you always, to the very end of the age." Matthew 28:18-20 (NIV)

Samuel Fiftieth Birthday

Rose Fiftieth Birthday

50th

Birthday Celebration

for

Evangelist Rhodessia (Rose) Strong

March 20, 1999
6:00 P.M.
1601 South 21 Avenue
Hollywood, Florida 33020

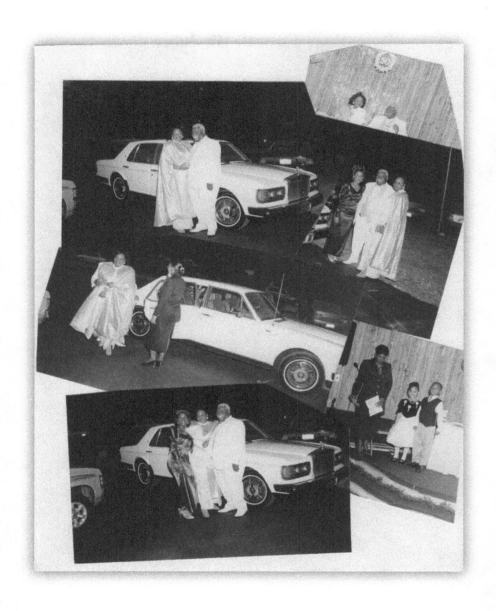

"Rhodessia"

Righteous, Rich and Rooted in God

Honest, Holy and Humble

Overcomer in Christ Jesus

Devoted to God, Husband, Family

Evangelistic and Equipped in God

Servant of the Most High God

Strong in the Lord and in the Power of His Might

Intercessor, Invading the kingdom of the devil

After the Heart of God

Favorite Colors

Blue... heavenly
Gold... perfection & integrity
Ivory Purple... wealth & living, royalty
White... victory, completion & God's glory

Her Interests

God's perfect and divine will be fulfilled in her life.
Reaching the total man regardless of religion, gender or race.

Mommy Dearest

To the mom I love whom no one can replace.
In which my heart will always have space.
For all the times you showed me you cared.
If no one else I knew, you'd be there.
Words can't express what I feel inside.
And my love for thee, I will never hide.
When you see me now, you can rest assured.
For Life's struggle has made me mature.
If I had one wish, Do you know what it will be?
That my dearest Mom live out all her dreams.

I Love You Mom
Your hard work payed off.

Samuel J. Strong III

Our Frist Granddaughter

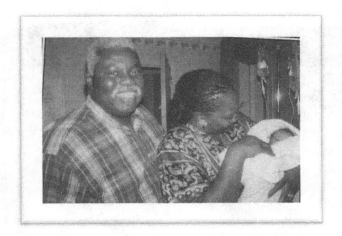

Family Dinner

Thirty-Two Years of Marriage

The Secret of Life
To My Loving Husband

I'm glad we took time to think together; it strengthened our relationship.

I'm glad we took time to pray and worship the Lord together in love.

I'm glad we took time to be friendly to each other; it was the road to the happiness we shared.

I'm glad we took time to work; it was the price of success.

I'm glad we took time to pray; it was the greatest power of the earth.

I'm glad we took time to forgive, for it strengthened our marriage.

I'm glad we took time to spend time together, for we experienced a true love.

I'm glad we took time to love and be loved, for it was the way of God.

Though I am glad, I will miss the door opening for your arrival at 4:15 p.m.

Though I am glad, I will miss watching the 10:00 o'clock news with you.

Thought I am glad, I will miss you letting out your recliner while I'm letting out mine.

Though I am glad, I will miss us shopping and doing all the things we enjoyed together.

Though I am glad, I will miss the path you made from your side of the bed to mine; it is fading.

Though I am glad, I will miss your embrace, your touch and your kiss...

Love, Your Rose!

Sampson

Tea`Ko

"The Priceless Gift God Gave for You"

This is how much God loved the world.
He gave his Son, his one and only Son.
And this is why; so that no one need
Be destroyed; by believing in him (Jesus).
Anyone can have a whole and lasting life.
God didn't go to all the trouble of sending
His Son merely to point an accusing finger,
Telling the world how bad it was. He came to help
To put the world right again. (John 3:16–17, MSG)

What Gift Will You Give God?

Please do not put off today for tomorrow just might be too late!

For what is a man profited, if he shall gain
the whole world, and lose his own soul?
Or what shall a man give in exchange for
his soul? (Matthew 16:26)

Please don't be like the rich man who lifts up his eyes in hell and could not escape. Please read Luke 16:19–31.

If my name is not written in the Book of Life, what will happen to me? Read Revelation 20:12–15.

Right now is the right time to prepare for heaven:

1. Believe the Word of God (John 3:36; Acts 16:31)
2. Repent, and turn from your sins (Luke 13:3)
3. Ask the Lord to save you (Romans 10:9–13)
4. Ask the Lord to fill you with his Spirit (Acts 1:8; Acts 2:2–6)
5. You should receive water baptism (Mark 1:8; Acts 2:38–39)
6. Studying the Bible (John is a great book to start your study)
7. Praying to God daily
8. Going to a Bible believing and Bible teaching Church
9. Telling someone about your new life in Christ Jesus

Comfort for the Believers in Christ

Praise the God and Father of our Lord Jesus Christ! He is the Father who is compassionate and the God who gives comfort. He comforts us whenever we suffer. That is why whenever other people suffer, we are able to comfort them by using the same comfort we have received from God. (2 Corinthians 1:3-4, GW)

I pray this will encourage you. It is not easy, but you will make it. Believe me, it will get better.

Be encouraged.
Love, Rose.

Rose's Prayer to the Almighty God

Lord, you have given me a great blessing
and an awesome responsibility.
Help me to be worthy!
Grant me the wisdom and ability;
To counsel wisely and well, strength
to practice what I preach
Courage to live always in your light
And grace to help lead others to you.
Let everything I do be done to glorify you
In Jesus' name, Amen!

You Are More Than A Conquer!

No, in all these things we are more than conquerors through him who loved us.[38] *For I am convinced that neither death nor life, neither angels nor demons,*[k] *neither the present nor the future, nor any powers,*[39] *neither height nor depth, nor anything else in all creation, will be able to separate us from the love of God that is in Christ Jesus our Lord.*
Romans 8:38-39 (NIV)

They triumphed over him by the blood of the Lamb and by the word of their testimony; they did not love their lives so much as to shrink from death.
Revelation 12:11

HEALING, DELIVERANCE, AND REFLECTIONS

God's Protection

In the late 1950s or early 1960s, growing up as an innocent little girl drinking from a water fountain, in America, Georgia, with a sign saying "White's only," I had no idea what could have happened to me. However, God protected my innocence and shielded me from the enemy.

Only God's Strength

In the 1950s, it was hard for me to forget how my mother worked from early mornings to late nights, laboring, so that her children could have a better life. She made so much sacrifice and paid such great price in paving the way for her children, grandchildren, and, today, even her great grandchildren.

Gods' favor?

In the late 1960s, my oldest brother Ruben, his fiancée Ann, and myself were on our way to Andersonville,

Georgia. We were driving in a 1957 Buick Central car. It was late in the night, and my brother fell asleep at the wheel; he was heading into a lake. I started screaming, alarming my soon-to-be sister-in-law who, in turn, woke my brother up. We were on our way to bring one of my second older sisters and her children to Miami for a visit. I later learned she was in a very abusive marriage. While in Andersonville, the transmission in my brother's car ran hot and had to be replaced. Up until this day, I am still trying to understand how eleven people fitted in that car that drove more than six hundred miles to Miami, without further problems. It is obvious that God had allowed his angels to encamp around us and that car. Those days, we definitely did not function out of fear but *faith*.

God's Shield

In 1968, while I was working as a cashier at A&G Markets, on my first real job, as customers checked out through my line, a man came through with a double barrel shotgun and pointed it at my face. He uttered a few words in a low-toned voice—I was so shocked. I was not aware that I was being robbed. Instinctively, another cashier shouted to me, "Give him the money, give him the money!!!" I did! Praise God for saving my life that day.

Romans 8:28 (GW) says, "We know that all things work together for the good of those who love God—those whom he has called according to his plan."

First Glimpse

Shortly after this horrible experience, something wonderful happened to me in that same grocery store that would shape my life for the future—I met this very handsome, neatly built young, dark-skinned man with curly black hair and pearly white teeth. I was the cashier; he was the bagboy. He appeared to be a very nice young man. He asked me, "What is your name, sweet thing?" I told him my name was Rhodessia. He had a difficult time pronouncing my name, so he started calling me "Rose." Weeks later, we courted for a while and soon fell in love. *Our love blossomed into marriage and a beautiful family.*

A Mighty Rushing Wind

This is an event I will never forget—my salvation testimony.

In 1971, I recalled one Friday night (approximately between 8:00 p.m. and 11:00 p.m.), I was listening to some songs from an album. I clearly remember sitting on a sofa chair with my daughter on my lap—I had purchased that chair from a thrift store; it was covered with a pink chenille bedspread. Somewhat relaxed, I listened and meditated on a particular gospel song entitled "Prayer (Vinyl LP)," by Rev. Ruben Willingham. As the music played, in my spirit, I found myself worshipping and thanking God, not really understanding or even realizing what was taking place in my life at the moment. Thank God for how he saved me that night (Rhodessia "Rose" Strong).

When the Enemy Said Yes, God Said No!

In 1972, several months after my son was born, the doctors diagnosed our son with spinal meningitis. Neither my husband nor I knew how serious it even was. Our son was hospitalized for several weeks. When my husband and I would visit him, it was extremely painful, as we were not allowed to pick him up or hug him. We surrounded his little bed, hoping for a miracle. As a mother, seeing so many tubes and/or wires hanging from his tiny little body; needles in his arms, hands, feet, and forehead; and machines beeping around his bed, was very devastating for me. Suddenly, it made me realize that this was really serious.

Whenever I would go to visit him, walking into that room and seeing him lying there in the same position was very devastating for me. At the time, I was a new Christian and I didn't know anything about spiritual warfare, praying in the spirit, or even calling someone else to pray with me. Ironically though, deep down inside, I could feel my reflecting back my spirit man rising up in me and making intercessions for my baby. I believed in God and that my baby would live and not die. That was my faith in action as a new Christian. Praise be to our Lord God almighty. He heard and answered my prayers. Our son was healed, and days later he was discharged from the hospital. Praise the Lord. God had a plan for my son's life. What the enemy meant for evil, God turned it around and worked it out for good—praise the Lord!

Near-Death Experience

During the mid-1970s, I will never forget my second sister becoming very ill and was hospitalized for quite some time. Whenever I would visit her, she could barely speak; she appeared to always be in despair and seemed very worried about her children. Although it was painful for me to see her fragile body, weighing less than one hundred pounds, hooked up to machines, heart monitors, and feeding tubes, in my heart I desired to see my sister healed and out of that hospital. Not knowing the Lord as how I came to know him later, in my heart I began to pray and lay hands on her. Miraculously, days later my sister started eating on her own. She even began to gain weight and was later discharged from the hospital. How can I forget those memorable moments with my sister? God almighty healed her and restored her back to health (Rhodessia "Rose" Strong).

The God Restoration

Again, in the late 1970s, another unusual but memorable event took place. My fifth older sibling's children were removed from their home and placed in another family member's care. To my knowledge, the family never understood the reason for the children's removal. Hence, she and her husband tried to regain custody. However, after a long battle with the court and state, the children were eventually placed in foster care. This action took a toll on both my sister and her husband mentally, emotionally, and physically.

Eventually, my sister had to be admitted to a state hospital for a period of time. I do recall visiting her and trying to stay in touch with her. However, after she was discharged, things got worse. Not knowing her children's whereabouts took an even stronger toll on her mentally and physically. For weeks and maybe months, neither her husband nor her family knew of her whereabouts. There were times when God would strongly place her on my heart and I would drive around for hours looking for her. I would not give up until I found her. When I saw the condition, she lived on the streets, I was moved with compassion. I showed her love and got her medical help and other needs. Today, I praise God my sister is alive, because I never gave up on her.

I don't recall how God did it, but he did! I was able to locate all of her children, except for one. They were all reunited with their mother in the late 1990s. By this time, they were all young adults. I am so grateful to God. Although it was not easy, because of God's grace and mercy, my sister is saved today. These are moments I cherish, because it has brought so much joy to our mother, myself, and other family members, some of whom are no longer with us (Rhodessia "Rose" Strong).

It Was Not My Time to Die

On December 7, 1973, at age 24, I was diagnosed with chronic pelvic inflammatory disease. I was admitted to the hospital for an operation. Prior to surgery, the doctors had explained the procedure to me which gave me some reassurance that everything would be alright. After the operation, the next thing I felt was someone slapping my face yelling, "Mrs. Strong, wake up, wake up." I don't recall responding. It seemed that I was far away. However, the next day when I eventually woke up, there were tubes, heart monitors, flashing lights, and intravenous attachments, along with doctors and nurses standing at the foot and side of my bed. They were all in amazement, looking but saying very little of what had happened. I was under the impression that was the norm after surgery. I was so wrong!

Later, the patient in the bed next to me sat up in her bed, looking and smiling with relief as she stated, "They called code blue on you last night. Doctors and nurses were trying to revive you." Looking back on that near-death experience, I can only say, it was not my time to slip into eternity. God had another plan for my life.

Again, on October 15, 1974, I was admitted to the JMH hospital with an ovarian cyst that required immediate surgery. Again, the enemy tried to destroy me, but God restored me (Rhodessia "Rose" Strong).

Jesus Saves

In the late 1970s, one of my sisters in the Lord and I shared the gospel and prayed with one of my oldest siblings. As a result, she accepted Christ in her life. In 2017, when her health began to fail, she and I shared some precious moments. Days before she departed from this life, the Spirit of God led me to serve her communion which she so looked forward to. Having made her peace with God, she waited patiently prior to her earthly departure. Now safe in the arms of Christ, it is comforting to know that she has found rest in the kingdom of God.

Less Than Six Hours to Live

February 8, 1983, awakened by excruciating abdominal pain, all I could do for relief was press my hands in my stomach and call on the name of Jesus. I was so weak. I could barely pull my head up—the pain was so severe. I felt as if my eyes were getting larger and I was far, far away. The doctor gave me less than six hours to live. Oh, but my God kept me! I was in the hospital for approximately eighteen days. Again, God restored me and gave me another chance (Rhodessia "Rose" Strong).

A Taste of Pentecost

Let me tell you about 1985! For years, I had stood in the gap for my late husband, confessing, speaking, and believing the Word of God on his behalf. When I least expected, God answered my prayers. The following Sunday, my husband went to the altar and openly confessed Jesus Christ as Lord in his life. Oh, what a time of rejoicing that was! The people began to praise and thank God for manifesting his Word. Several weeks later, he and I began sharing the Word of God, seriously studying from the Book of Acts, chapters 1 and 2. Looking each other in the face, I asked my husband, "Do you want to be filled with the Holy Spirit?"

He answered, "Yes!" He and I went to our bedroom; as soon as he knelt, the Holy Spirit came upon him and he began to speak in his heavenly language—hallelujah! How can I forget that glorious moment *seeing the awesome presence of God overshadow my husband?*

Later, my *fourth* brother met the love of his life, accepted Christ, and got married, and they both served faithfully for the kingdom, together.

The Word of God Will Change You

John 8:32 (GW) says, "You will know the truth, and the truth will set you free."

Here's another extraordinary event that I cherished. One of my family members had been cohabitating for many years. God placed on my heart and my husband's (Samuel J. Strong Jr.) heart to go and share scriptures with them concerning marriage. I joined my husband in sharing briefly that we were in the same situation, that no one told us we were living in sin, and that neither did we have any biblical knowledge about marriage. It was after I accepted Jesus as my Lord and savior I realized we need to get married. After hearing our testimony, praise God, thank you, Jesus, they got married and lived happily ever after. Unfortunately, the wife departed this earthly life in January 2016. Thank God we obeyed the voice of God.

Will You Pay the Cost?

August 1995, seeking God for seven days on a trip in Atlanta, Georgia, the Lord placed it on my heart to go and share the gospel of Jesus Christ with my niece who lived in Oglethorpe, Georgia. After sharing with my roommate and another sister who attended the meeting what the Lord laid on my heart, that sister agreed to drive me and my roommate to Oglethorpe, Georgia—which was a two-hour drive away—to share the gospel with my niece. I am so glad we followed the voice of God. My niece accepted the Lord as her Lord and savior, and in October 2017, she went home to be with to be with the Lord.

It is so important that when God gives us an opportunity to share the gospel with others, it is vital that we follow God's plan because we never know what could happen. Praise God, it was worth the drive, the time, and a testimony.

Glorious Day!

Wednesday, August 13, 1997, my mother had no appetite; she just wanted to rest. She had gotten very weak; her last steps were between 10:00 a.m. and 11:00 a.m. I sat by my mother's bedside, pinning hankies together. Holding her hand and talking with her as she lay in bed, I asked her, "Mother, are you getting ready for heaven?"

Grabbing the cover on the bed and pulling herself up, she said, "Yes! I'm going to see Jesus!"

I asked her, "Are you going to leave me?"

Again, she said, "Yes! I'm going to see Jesus, honey!" There was so much joy in her expression and peace on her face as she lay in bed looking upward as if she had seen angels or glorious/heaven.

On August 16 between 7:10 a.m. and 7:15 a.m., Mother went home to be with our Lord. 2 Corinthians 5:8 (KJV) says, "We are confident, *I say*, and willing rather to be absent from the body and to be present with the Lord."

Desiring Change

Psalm 105:4 (KJV) says, "Seek the *Lord*, and his strength: seek his face evermore."

In year 2002, there was another unforgettable moment. During that year, we were holding church services at an elementary school. One Sunday, one of my precious great nieces and her daughter attended worship service, heard and believed the Word of God, and, as a result, gave their lives to the Lord and continued to serve him faithfully in the ministry. Some families called it "the family church," as many family members attended services with us there and heard and received the Words of God. I treasure these moments!

God Never Said It Would Be Easy

In *2004,* I value the time my late husband and I served together in ministry for many years. We witnessed how God supernaturally changed many lives. We also experienced the presence of God in our marriage, family, and "evening of romance," and seeing many marriages restored was also unexplainable!!!

Oh, the Joy!

In *2005,* my second older sister accepted Christ as her Lord and savior; she attended Solid Rock Redemptive Ministries faithfully. It was a great joy seeing my sister loving and worshipping God in her golden years. Along with her, several of her children and grandchildren also attended church with her. During the times when she was unable to attend service, my visits with her were precious moments that I often reflected upon. Her departure from this life, on December 31, 2014, was truly a home-going service.

Jesus Heals

Jesus went to all the towns and villages. He taught in the synagogues and spread the good news of the kingdom. He also cured every disease and sickness.

—Matthew 9:35 (GW)

In the year 2015, one of my nieces was hospitalized for several weeks. When I would go to visit her, I could see the spirit of death trying to take over. The physical pain was so obvious, she could not even speak. As I prayed for her, I could see that she wanted to live. My sister-in-law and I went to the hospital, anointed her with oil, and laid hands on her, and days later she was discharged. So joyful, again, that I obeyed the voice of God.

In 2016 thru 2017, when it seemed in the natural that my oldest brother would not make it through many operations, my fourth brother and I went to the hospital, stood in agreement in prayer, and God healed my brother. To God we give all the glory!

In 2017, my third oldest sister had a stroke and was taken to the hospital. The doctors advised that she would not be able to eat regular foods and would need to be fed through a feeding tube. She and I agreed in fervent prayers and days later she was discharged from the hospital. She has since been eating regular foods and now has resumed regular activities. Praise God! Not only is he a healer, he also restores!

Along with all of the above, there are many more significant events that happened around and within my entire family circle and other people that I recall and treasure. Families are created by God to love and bear one *another's burdens*!!!

Rhodessia "Rose" Strong is the president and founder of Solid Rock Redemptive Ministries, Inc. and Urban and Community Outreach Squad (UCOS) a division of Solid Rock Redemptive Ministries. Rose is a very talented and blessed woman of God. She continues to demonstrate a spirit of compassion for the lost and those who are hurting, abused, and rejected, specializing in children and families.

Rose is a very family- and community-oriented person who is well-versed in various areas including, but not limited to, ministerial counseling, neighborhoods/family workshops and seminars, street meetings, hospitals and nursing home activities, and VIA radio host. She is no stranger to outreach programs when it comes to food, shelter, clothing distribution, and educational and healthcare workshops in the South Florida region. She has also ministered the gospel through fashion shows in Miami Dade County public schools, churches, and other events. In earlier times, Rose and her late husband (Elder Samuel J. Strong Jr.) directed an event entitled "Evening of Romance" that celebrated and strengthened marriages.

As a *crisis intervention therapist*, she worked with neglected, abused, and abandoned children and families in the Miami Dade/Monroe County areas. She has a heart for "at-risk" individuals, families, children, and youth. She continues to witness to and mentor countless number of people in need to get the help they needed.

The future of our younger generation is of major concern to Rose. Her mission is to see our youth use their talents constructively, instead of destructively. She recognizes the potential and visions of our children and feels compelled to help them fulfill their needs.

Now visually-impaired, she refuses to allow a disability to hinder her capability to help bring change to neighborhoods, schools, communities and cities. She endeavors to reach the total man through compassion, love, and faith in God.

Education:

1. The nurturing parenting program facilitator: 2007, the nurturing parenting programs
2. M.S. marriage and family therapy: 2003, St. Thomas University
3. B.A. interpersonal and group communications: 2000, Trinity International University
4. A.S. fashion designing: 1978, Miami Dade Community College, and *numerous certification*

My delights:

1. Sharing the gospel, Counseling others and referring them to other agencies when needed
2. Designing/sewing clothes
3. Fashion exhibits to help particularly our younger generation enhance their talents

Pleasures:

1. Attending and volunteering at church
2. Listening to Christian music/studying the Bible
3. Cooking and baking, sharing the gospel and winning souls for the Kingdom of God.